A FOOD
JOURNAL

DISCLAIMER

✕ ✕ ✕

WE'VE BEEN LUCKY ENOUGH TO HAVE
HAD THE OPPORTUNITY TO EAT AT SOME
AMAZING PLACES OVER THE COURSE OF
OUR LIVES SO FAR. SO MUCH SO, THAT
IT'S OFTEN HARD TO REMEMBER THEM
ALL. OKAY, A FEW DRINKS MIGHT ALSO
BE PARTLY TO BLAME.

REGARDLESS, THAT'S WHY WE MADE THIS.
A FOOD JOURNAL FOR PEOPLE WHO
REALLY LOVE FOOD. WHICH IS EVERYONE—
OR AT LEAST IT SHOULD BE. USE IT TO
MEMORIALIZE (AND FIND) ALL OF THOSE
AMAZING, HIDDEN-GEM PLACES THAT YOU
STUMBLE UPON—EITHER WHILE TRAVELING,
OR IN YOUR OWN TOWN.

AS A BONUS, WE'VE INCLUDED A TRAVEL
GUIDE OF SORTS. SPRINKLED THROUGHOUT,
YOU'LL FIND A FEW (OKAY, SEVERAL) OF
OUR FAVORITES. NO MATTER THE CATEGORY
YOU'LL FIND A RANGE OF PRICE-POINTS,
FOOD STYLES, AND AESTHETICS—BECAUSE
WE'RE ECLECTIC TO SAY THE LEAST.

THAT SAID, WHILE WE TRIED OUR BEST
TO MAKE SURE THAT EVERY RESTAURANT
IS UP-TO-DATE (AND STILL IN BUSINESS),
THE FOOD WORLD IS A FICKLE PLACE.
IT'S INEVITABLE THAT A FEW OF THESE
PLACES MAY NO LONGER BE WITH US AT
SOME POINT. PLEASE DON'T YELL AT US.

@ BRASSMONKEYGOODS

AN EXAMPLE RESTAURANT

NAME OF THE RESTAURANT

WESTSIDE LOCAL

NUMBER

723

PSST: ADD THIS TO THE INDEX(ES) IN THE BACK SO YOU CAN FIND IT QUICKLY LATER

WHERE WAS IT LOCATED?

CITY: KANSAS CITY STATE/COUNTRY: MISSOURI

WHY DID YOU EAT HERE?

- ☒ HEARD GREAT THINGS
- ☐ IT LOOKED GOOD
- ☐ ONLY THING OPEN
- ☐ FORCED AGAINST WILL
- ☐ HUNGRY & DESPERATE
- ☐ WAS DRUNK

OTHER:

THE BEST THING(S) YOU ATE:

Deviled Eggs, ELOTE TATER TOTS & the STEAK SALAD

THE WORST THING(S) YOU ATE:

* NOTHING *

AMBIANCE
① ② ③ ④ ⊗

FOOD
① ② ③ ④ ⊗

SERVICE
① ② ③ ④ ⊗

THE ONE THING YOU'LL NEVER FORGET:

OVERHEARING A *pretentious* CONVERSATION ABOUT MUSIC. (EYE ROLL)

EAT HERE AGAIN? YES ☒ NO ☐ IF DESPERATE ☐

HOW TO USE THIS BOOK

BELOW YOU'LL FIND A LIST OF THE VARIOUS 'CATEGORIES' OF RESTAURANTS IN THIS BOOK—INTERPRET THESE HOWEVER YOU SEE FIT, THIS IS YOUR BOOK AFTER ALL. SIMPLY GO EAT SOMEWHERE & FLIP TO THE MOST SUITABLE CATEGORY. FIND AN OPEN PAGE, AND WRITE ABOUT YOUR EXPERIENCE (SEE AN EXAMPLE TO THE LEFT).

THE UNIQUE NUMBER ON THAT PAGE NOW BELONGS TO THAT RESTAURANT (TO FIND IT LATER). SO FLIP TO THE VARIOUS INDEX PAGES IN THE BACK AND ADD IT TO AS MANY LISTS AS YOU SEE FIT (LIKE BELOW). BEST MEXICAN PLACE? ADD IT. ONE OF THE BEST PLACES IN MAINE? ADD IT. TERRIBLE? DON'T ADD IT ANYWHERE & FORGET THAT PLACE EVER EXISTED.

RESTAURANT   **NUMBER**

WESTSIDE LOCAL   723

CITY KANSAS CITY, MO   RATING ① ② ③ ④ ⊗

RESTAURANT CATEGORY	NUMBER RANGE
BREAKFAST & BRUNCH	001-030
FOOD TRUCKS, CARTS, & STANDS	031-060
DIVES, DINERS, & GREASY SPOONS	061-090
HIPSTER SPOTS & TRENDY PLACES	091-120
CHAIN RESTAURANTS (OF ALL SIZES)	121-150
FINE DINING & OTHER FANCY PLACES	151-180
BARS & SPEAKEASIES	181-210
ICE CREAM & DESSERT SPOTS	211-240
INDEX PAGES	ALL OF THE REST

IN MORNING

IN MORNING

AKA: BREAKFAST & BRUNCH

NAME OF THE RESTAURANT

NUMBER

001

PSST: ADD THIS TO THE INDEX(ES) IN THE BACK SO YOU CAN FIND IT QUICKLY LATER

WHERE WAS IT LOCATED?

CITY: STATE/COUNTRY:

WHY DID YOU EAT HERE?

☐ HEARD GREAT THINGS   FORCED AGAINST WILL ☐

☐ IT LOOKED GOOD   HUNGRY & DESPERATE ☐

☐ ONLY THING OPEN   WAS DRUNK ☐

OTHER:

THE BEST THING(S) YOU ATE:

. . . .

THE WORST THING(S) YOU ATE:

. . . .

AMBIANCE
① ② ③ ④ ⑤

FOOD
① ② ③ ④ ⑤

SERVICE
① ② ③ ④ ⑤

THE ONE THING YOU'LL NEVER FORGET:

EAT HERE AGAIN?   YES ☐   NO ☐   IF DESPERATE ☐

IN MORNING

NUMBER

002

NAME OF THE RESTAURANT

PSST: ADD THIS TO THE INDEX(ES) IN THE BACK SO YOU CAN FIND IT QUICKLY LATER

WHERE WAS IT LOCATED?

CITY:

STATE/COUNTRY:

WHY DID YOU EAT HERE?

☐ HEARD GREAT THINGS

☐ IT LOOKED GOOD

☐ ONLY THING OPEN

FORCED AGAINST WILL ☐

HUNGRY & DESPERATE ☐

WAS DRUNK ☐

OTHER:

AMBIANCE

① ② ③ ④ ⑤

FOOD

① ② ③ ④ ⑤

SERVICE

① ② ③ ④ ⑤

THE BEST THING(S) YOU ATE:

. . . .

THE WORST THING(S) YOU ATE:

. . . .

THE ONE THING YOU'LL NEVER FORGET:

EAT HERE AGAIN? YES ☐ NO ☐ IF DESPERATE ☐

IN MORNING

AKA: BREAKFAST & BRUNCH

NAME OF THE RESTAURANT

NUMBER

003

PSST: ADD THIS TO THE INDEX(ES) IN THE BACK SO YOU CAN FIND IT QUICKLY LATER

WHERE WAS IT LOCATED?

CITY: STATE/COUNTRY:

WHY DID YOU EAT HERE?

☐ HEARD GREAT THINGS   FORCED AGAINST WILL ☐

☐ IT LOOKED GOOD   HUNGRY & DESPERATE ☐

☐ ONLY THING OPEN   WAS DRUNK ☐

OTHER:

THE BEST THING(S) YOU ATE:

. . . .

THE WORST THING(S) YOU ATE:

. . . .

AMBIANCE

① ② ③ ④ ⑤

FOOD

① ② ③ ④ ⑤

SERVICE

① ② ③ ④ ⑤

THE ONE THING YOU'LL NEVER FORGET:

EAT HERE AGAIN?   YES ☐   NO ☐   IF DESPERATE ☐

IN MORNING

NUMBER

004

NAME OF THE RESTAURANT

PSST: ADD THIS TO THE INDEX(ES) IN THE BACK SO YOU CAN FIND IT QUICKLY LATER

WHERE WAS IT LOCATED?

CITY: STATE/COUNTRY:

WHY DID YOU EAT HERE?

- [ ] HEARD GREAT THINGS
- [ ] IT LOOKED GOOD
- [ ] ONLY THING OPEN

- FORCED AGAINST WILL [ ]
- HUNGRY & DESPERATE [ ]
- WAS DRUNK [ ]

OTHER:

AMBIANCE
(1) (2) (3) (4) (5)

FOOD
(1) (2) (3) (4) (5)

SERVICE
(1) (2) (3) (4) (5)

THE BEST THING(S) YOU ATE:
. . . .

THE WORST THING(S) YOU ATE:
. . . .

THE ONE THING YOU'LL NEVER FORGET:

EAT HERE AGAIN?   YES [ ]   NO [ ]   IF DESPERATE [ ]

IN MORNING

NAME OF THE RESTAURANT

NUMBER

005

PSST: ADD THIS TO THE INDEX(ES) IN THE BACK SO YOU CAN FIND IT QUICKLY LATER

WHERE WAS IT LOCATED?

CITY: STATE/COUNTRY:

WHY DID YOU EAT HERE?

- [ ] HEARD GREAT THINGS
- [ ] IT LOOKED GOOD
- [ ] ONLY THING OPEN
- [ ] FORCED AGAINST WILL
- [ ] HUNGRY & DESPERATE
- [ ] WAS DRUNK

OTHER:

THE BEST THING(S) YOU ATE:

. . . .

THE WORST THING(S) YOU ATE:

. . . .

AMBIANCE
(1) (2) (3) (4) (5)

FOOD
(1) (2) (3) (4) (5)

SERVICE
(1) (2) (3) (4) (5)

THE ONE THING YOU'LL NEVER FORGET:

EAT HERE AGAIN?   YES [ ]   NO [ ]   IF DESPERATE [ ]

NUMBER

006

NAME OF THE RESTAURANT

PSST: ADD THIS TO THE INDEX(ES) IN THE BACK SO YOU CAN FIND IT QUICKLY LATER

WHERE WAS IT LOCATED?

CITY: STATE/COUNTRY:

WHY DID YOU EAT HERE?

☐ HEARD GREAT THINGS   FORCED AGAINST WILL ☐

☐ IT LOOKED GOOD   HUNGRY & DESPERATE ☐

☐ ONLY THING OPEN   WAS DRUNK ☐

OTHER:

AMBIANCE

① ② ③ ④ ⑤

FOOD

① ② ③ ④ ⑤

SERVICE

① ② ③ ④ ⑤

THE BEST THING(S) YOU ATE:

. . . .

THE WORST THING(S) YOU ATE:

. . . .

THE ONE THING YOU'LL NEVER FORGET:

EAT HERE AGAIN?   YES ☐   NO ☐   IF DESPERATE ☐

NAME OF THE RESTAURANT

NUMBER

007

PSST: ADD THIS TO THE INDEX(ES) IN THE BACK SO YOU CAN FIND IT QUICKLY LATER

WHERE WAS IT LOCATED?

CITY: STATE/COUNTRY:

WHY DID YOU EAT HERE?

- [ ] HEARD GREAT THINGS
- [ ] IT LOOKED GOOD
- [ ] ONLY THING OPEN
- [ ] FORCED AGAINST WILL
- [ ] HUNGRY & DESPERATE
- [ ] WAS DRUNK

OTHER:

THE BEST THING(S) YOU ATE:

. . . .

AMBIANCE
① ② ③ ④ ⑤

FOOD
① ② ③ ④ ⑤

THE WORST THING(S) YOU ATE:

. . . .

SERVICE
① ② ③ ④ ⑤

THE ONE THING YOU'LL NEVER FORGET:

EAT HERE AGAIN?   YES ☐   NO ☐   IF DESPERATE ☐

OUR FAVORITES

☐ BEEN THERE

SHOPSIN'S

88 ESSEX STREET, NEW YORK, NY 10002

A FEW SPECIALTIES

☐ MAC & CHEESE PANCAKES

☐ THE SANTANA PETE

☐ LITERALLY EVERYTHING ELSE

POACHED EGGS

① ② ③ ④ ⑤

PROFANITY

① ② ③ ④ ⑤

IF WE'RE BEING HONEST—WE KNOW A LITTLE TOO MUCH ABOUT THIS PLACE. HANDS DOWN, THIS IS ONE OF OUR FAVORITE RESTAURANTS IN THE WORLD. IT WAS STARTED BY KENNY & EVE SHOPSIN IN 1973 AS A GENERAL STORE— BUT IT TURNED INTO SO MUCH MORE. SADLY KENNY & EVE HAVE SINCE PASSED AWAY, BUT THEIR LEGACY LIVES ON THROUGH THEIR KIDS THAT STILL RUN IT. SURE, THEY WON'T CUSS YOU OUT NEAR AS MUCH—BUT THE AMAZING FOOD HASN'T CHANGED ONE BIT.

☐ BEEN THERE

ODDLY CORRECT

4141 TROOST AVE, KANSAS CITY, MO 64110

A FEW SPECIALTIES

☐ POUR-OVER COFFEE

☐ BREAKFAST SANDWICHES

☐ HOUSE-MADE BISCUITS

COFFEE QUALITY

① ② ③ ④ ⑤

AMPLE SEATING

① ② ③ ④ ⑤

THIS PLACE MAKES THE BEST COFFEE WE'VE EVER HAD. IN FACT, THEY'VE SINGLE-HANDEDLY TURNED US ALL INTO A BUNCH OF COFFEE SNOBS. THEY SOURCE & ROAST THEIR OWN BEANS—WHICH THEY SELL IN BAGS ONLINE AND IN LOCAL STORES. IN FACT, IT'S PRETTY MUCH THE ONLY THING WE DRINK HERE IN OUR OFFICE. HOWEVER, THEIR CAFE REALLY SEALS THE DEAL—WITH AMAZING BISCUIT SANDWICHES MADE FROM SCRATCH EVERYDAY. WE'VE BEEN MAINSTAYS THERE FOR 10+ YEARS.

IN MORNING

AKA: BREAKFAST & BRUNCH

NAME OF THE RESTAURANT

NUMBER

008

PSST: ADD THIS TO THE INDEX(ES) IN THE BACK SO YOU CAN FIND IT QUICKLY LATER

WHERE WAS IT LOCATED?

CITY: STATE/COUNTRY:

WHY DID YOU EAT HERE?

- [ ] HEARD GREAT THINGS
- [ ] IT LOOKED GOOD
- [ ] ONLY THING OPEN
- [ ] FORCED AGAINST WILL
- [ ] HUNGRY & DESPERATE
- [ ] WAS DRUNK

OTHER:

THE BEST THING(S) YOU ATE:

. . . .

AMBIANCE
(1) (2) (3) (4) (5)

FOOD
(1) (2) (3) (4) (5)

THE WORST THING(S) YOU ATE:

. . . .

SERVICE
(1) (2) (3) (4) (5)

THE ONE THING YOU'LL NEVER FORGET:

EAT HERE AGAIN? YES [ ] NO [ ] IF DESPERATE [ ]

NUMBER

009

NAME OF THE RESTAURANT

PSST: ADD THIS TO THE INDEX(ES) IN THE BACK SO YOU CAN FIND IT QUICKLY LATER

WHERE WAS IT LOCATED?

CITY: STATE/COUNTRY:

WHY DID YOU EAT HERE?

- [ ] HEARD GREAT THINGS
- [ ] IT LOOKED GOOD
- [ ] ONLY THING OPEN

FORCED AGAINST WILL [ ]
HUNGRY & DESPERATE [ ]
WAS DRUNK [ ]

OTHER:

AMBIANCE
① ② ③ ④ ⑤

FOOD
① ② ③ ④ ⑤

SERVICE
① ② ③ ④ ⑤

THE BEST THING(S) YOU ATE:

. . . .

THE WORST THING(S) YOU ATE:

. . . .

THE ONE THING YOU'LL NEVER FORGET:

EAT HERE AGAIN?   YES [ ]   NO [ ]   IF DESPERATE [ ]

NAME OF THE RESTAURANT

NUMBER

010

PSST: ADD THIS TO THE INDEX(ES) IN THE BACK SO YOU CAN FIND IT QUICKLY LATER

WHERE WAS IT LOCATED?

CITY: STATE/COUNTRY:

WHY DID YOU EAT HERE?

- [ ] HEARD GREAT THINGS
- [ ] IT LOOKED GOOD
- [ ] ONLY THING OPEN
- [ ] FORCED AGAINST WILL
- [ ] HUNGRY & DESPERATE
- [ ] WAS DRUNK

OTHER:

THE BEST THING(S) YOU ATE:

. . . .

THE WORST THING(S) YOU ATE:

. . . .

AMBIANCE
① ② ③ ④ ⑤

FOOD
① ② ③ ④ ⑤

SERVICE
① ② ③ ④ ⑤

THE ONE THING YOU'LL NEVER FORGET:

EAT HERE AGAIN? YES [ ] NO [ ] IF DESPERATE [ ]

NUMBER

011

NAME OF THE RESTAURANT

PSST: ADD THIS TO THE INDEX(ES) IN THE BACK SO YOU CAN FIND IT QUICKLY LATER

WHERE WAS IT LOCATED?

CITY: STATE/COUNTRY:

WHY DID YOU EAT HERE?

☐ HEARD GREAT THINGS   FORCED AGAINST WILL ☐

☐ IT LOOKED GOOD   HUNGRY & DESPERATE ☐

☐ ONLY THING OPEN   WAS DRUNK ☐

OTHER:

AMBIANCE
① ② ③ ④ ⑤

THE BEST THING(S) YOU ATE:
. . . .

FOOD
① ② ③ ④ ⑤

THE WORST THING(S) YOU ATE:
. . . .

SERVICE
① ② ③ ④ ⑤

THE ONE THING YOU'LL NEVER FORGET:

EAT HERE AGAIN?   YES ☐   NO ☐   IF DESPERATE ☐

IN MORNING

NAME OF THE RESTAURANT

NUMBER

012

PSST: ADD THIS TO THE INDEX(ES) IN THE BACK SO YOU CAN FIND IT QUICKLY LATER

WHERE WAS IT LOCATED?

CITY: STATE/COUNTRY:

WHY DID YOU EAT HERE?

☐ HEARD GREAT THINGS   FORCED AGAINST WILL ☐

☐ IT LOOKED GOOD   HUNGRY & DESPERATE ☐

☐ ONLY THING OPEN   WAS DRUNK ☐

OTHER:

THE BEST THING(S) YOU ATE:

. . . .

THE WORST THING(S) YOU ATE:

. . . .

AMBIANCE
① ② ③ ④ ⑤

FOOD
① ② ③ ④ ⑤

SERVICE
① ② ③ ④ ⑤

THE ONE THING YOU'LL NEVER FORGET:

EAT HERE AGAIN?   YES ☐   NO ☐   IF DESPERATE ☐

NUMBER

013

NAME OF THE RESTAURANT

PSST: ADD THIS TO THE INDEX(ES) IN THE BACK SO YOU CAN FIND IT QUICKLY LATER

WHERE WAS IT LOCATED?

CITY: STATE/COUNTRY:

WHY DID YOU EAT HERE?

- [ ] HEARD GREAT THINGS
- [ ] IT LOOKED GOOD
- [ ] ONLY THING OPEN

- FORCED AGAINST WILL [ ]
- HUNGRY & DESPERATE [ ]
- WAS DRUNK [ ]

OTHER:

AMBIANCE
① ② ③ ④ ⑤

FOOD
① ② ③ ④ ⑤

SERVICE
① ② ③ ④ ⑤

THE BEST THING(S) YOU ATE:

. . . .

THE WORST THING(S) YOU ATE:

. . . .

THE ONE THING YOU'LL NEVER FORGET:

EAT HERE AGAIN?   YES [ ]   NO [ ]   IF DESPERATE [ ]

IN MORNING

NAME OF THE RESTAURANT

NUMBER

014

PSST: ADD THIS TO THE INDEX(ES) IN THE BACK SO YOU CAN FIND IT QUICKLY LATER

WHERE WAS IT LOCATED?

CITY: STATE/COUNTRY:

WHY DID YOU EAT HERE?

- [ ] HEARD GREAT THINGS
- [ ] IT LOOKED GOOD
- [ ] ONLY THING OPEN
- [ ] FORCED AGAINST WILL
- [ ] HUNGRY & DESPERATE
- [ ] WAS DRUNK

OTHER:

THE BEST THING(S) YOU ATE:

. . . .

THE WORST THING(S) YOU ATE:

. . . .

AMBIANCE
(1) (2) (3) (4) (5)

FOOD
(1) (2) (3) (4) (5)

SERVICE
(1) (2) (3) (4) (5)

THE ONE THING YOU'LL NEVER FORGET:

EAT HERE AGAIN?   YES [ ]   NO [ ]   IF DESPERATE [ ]

THE BLOODY MARY

NATIONAL BLOODY MARY DAY IS ON JANUARY 1ST

PERFECT FOR

- [ ] CURING HANGOVERS
- [ ] CREATING HANGOVERS

TERRIBLE FOR

- GENERAL PRODUCTIVITY [ ]
- SODIUM INTAKE [ ]

ALLEGEDLY, THE UBIQUITOUS CELERY STICK GARNISH ALL STARTED IN THE 1960s AS AN ACCIDENT. WHEN A CUSTOMER AT 'BUTCH MCGUIRE'S' IN CHICAGO DIDN'T GET A SWIZZLE STICK, THEY GRABBED A NEARBY CELERY STICK TO MIX THEIR DRINK. OTHER PATRONS IN THE BAR NOTICED—AND SOON THE CUSTOM WAS BORN.

FIND NOTABLES AT:

LOCATION

- [ ] MAISON PREMIERE — BROOKLYN, NY
- [ ] PRUBECHU — SAN FRANCISCO, CA
- [ ] BLANCHE BAR & RESTAURANT — KARRATHA, AUSTRALIA
- [ ] SUNDA — CHICAGO, IL
- [ ] CASINO EL CAMINO — AUSTIN, TX
- [ ] DANTE NYC — NEW YORK, NY
- [ ] STINGRAY'S GRILL AND BAR — NEW ORLEANS, LA
- [ ] SPOON AND STABLE — MINNEAPOLIS, MN
- [ ] SCORE ON DAVIE — VANCOUVER, CANADA
- [ ] BOSTONIA PUBLIC HOUSE — BOSTON, MA
- [ ] THE ATTIC — LONG BEACH, CA
- [ ] GENIE'S CAFE — PORTLAND, OR

WRITE-IN CANDIDATES

IN MORNING

NAME OF THE RESTAURANT

NUMBER

015

PSST: ADD THIS TO THE INDEX(ES) IN THE BACK SO YOU CAN FIND IT QUICKLY LATER

WHERE WAS IT LOCATED?

CITY: STATE/COUNTRY:

WHY DID YOU EAT HERE?

- [ ] HEARD GREAT THINGS
- [ ] IT LOOKED GOOD
- [ ] ONLY THING OPEN
- [ ] FORCED AGAINST WILL
- [ ] HUNGRY & DESPERATE
- [ ] WAS DRUNK

OTHER:

THE BEST THING(S) YOU ATE:
. . . .

THE WORST THING(S) YOU ATE:
. . . .

AMBIANCE
(1) (2) (3) (4) (5)

FOOD
(1) (2) (3) (4) (5)

SERVICE
(1) (2) (3) (4) (5)

THE ONE THING YOU'LL NEVER FORGET:

EAT HERE AGAIN?   YES [ ]   NO [ ]   IF DESPERATE [ ]

NUMBER

016

NAME OF THE RESTAURANT

PSST: ADD THIS TO THE INDEX(ES) IN THE BACK SO YOU CAN FIND IT QUICKLY LATER

WHERE WAS IT LOCATED?

CITY: STATE/COUNTRY:

WHY DID YOU EAT HERE?

☐ HEARD GREAT THINGS   FORCED AGAINST WILL ☐

☐ IT LOOKED GOOD   HUNGRY & DESPERATE ☐

☐ ONLY THING OPEN   WAS DRUNK ☐

OTHER:

AMBIANCE
① ② ③ ④ ⑤

FOOD
① ② ③ ④ ⑤

SERVICE
① ② ③ ④ ⑤

THE BEST THING(S) YOU ATE:

. . . .

THE WORST THING(S) YOU ATE:

. . . .

THE ONE THING YOU'LL NEVER FORGET:

EAT HERE AGAIN?   YES ☐   NO ☐   IF DESPERATE ☐

IN MORNING

NAME OF THE RESTAURANT

NUMBER

017

PSST: ADD THIS TO THE INDEX(ES) IN THE BACK SO YOU CAN FIND IT QUICKLY LATER

WHERE WAS IT LOCATED?

CITY: STATE/COUNTRY:

WHY DID YOU EAT HERE?

- [ ] HEARD GREAT THINGS
- [ ] IT LOOKED GOOD
- [ ] ONLY THING OPEN
- [ ] FORCED AGAINST WILL
- [ ] HUNGRY & DESPERATE
- [ ] WAS DRUNK

OTHER:

THE BEST THING(S) YOU ATE:

. . . .

AMBIANCE
① ② ③ ④ ⑤

FOOD
① ② ③ ④ ⑤

THE WORST THING(S) YOU ATE:

. . . .

SERVICE
① ② ③ ④ ⑤

THE ONE THING YOU'LL NEVER FORGET:

EAT HERE AGAIN?   YES [ ]   NO [ ]   IF DESPERATE [ ]

NUMBER

O18

NAME OF THE RESTAURANT

PSST: ADD THIS TO THE INDEX(ES) IN THE BACK SO YOU CAN FIND IT QUICKLY LATER

WHERE WAS IT LOCATED?

CITY: STATE/COUNTRY:

WHY DID YOU EAT HERE?

☐ HEARD GREAT THINGS   FORCED AGAINST WILL ☐

☐ IT LOOKED GOOD   HUNGRY & DESPERATE ☐

☐ ONLY THING OPEN   WAS DRUNK ☐

OTHER:

AMBIANCE
① ② ③ ④ ⑤

FOOD
① ② ③ ④ ⑤

SERVICE
① ② ③ ④ ⑤

THE BEST THING(S) YOU ATE:

. . . .

THE WORST THING(S) YOU ATE:

. . . .

THE ONE THING YOU'LL NEVER FORGET:

EAT HERE AGAIN?   YES ☐   NO ☐   IF DESPERATE ☐

IN MORNING

AKA: BREAKFAST & BRUNCH

NAME OF THE RESTAURANT

NUMBER

019

PSST: ADD THIS TO THE INDEX(ES) IN THE BACK SO YOU CAN FIND IT QUICKLY LATER

WHERE WAS IT LOCATED?

CITY: STATE/COUNTRY:

WHY DID YOU EAT HERE?

- [ ] HEARD GREAT THINGS
- [ ] IT LOOKED GOOD
- [ ] ONLY THING OPEN
- [ ] FORCED AGAINST WILL
- [ ] HUNGRY & DESPERATE
- [ ] WAS DRUNK

OTHER:

THE BEST THING(S) YOU ATE:

....

AMBIANCE
① ② ③ ④ ⑤

FOOD
① ② ③ ④ ⑤

THE WORST THING(S) YOU ATE:

....

SERVICE
① ② ③ ④ ⑤

THE ONE THING YOU'LL NEVER FORGET:

EAT HERE AGAIN?   YES [ ]   NO [ ]   IF DESPERATE [ ]

NUMBER   **NAME OF THE RESTAURANT**

020

PSST: ADD THIS TO THE INDEX(ES) IN THE BACK SO YOU CAN FIND IT QUICKLY LATER

WHERE WAS IT LOCATED?

CITY: STATE/COUNTRY:

WHY DID YOU EAT HERE?

☐ HEARD GREAT THINGS   FORCED AGAINST WILL ☐

☐ IT LOOKED GOOD   HUNGRY & DESPERATE ☐

☐ ONLY THING OPEN   WAS DRUNK ☐

OTHER:

AMBIANCE   **THE BEST THING(S) YOU ATE:**

① ② ③ ④ ⑤

. . . .

FOOD

① ② ③ ④ ⑤   **THE WORST THING(S) YOU ATE:**

SERVICE

① ② ③ ④ ⑤   . . . .

THE ONE THING YOU'LL NEVER FORGET:

EAT HERE AGAIN?   YES ☐   NO ☐   IF DESPERATE ☐

IN MORNING

NAME OF THE RESTAURANT

NUMBER

021

PSST: ADD THIS TO THE INDEX(ES) IN THE BACK SO YOU CAN FIND IT QUICKLY LATER

WHERE WAS IT LOCATED?

CITY: STATE/COUNTRY:

WHY DID YOU EAT HERE?

- [ ] HEARD GREAT THINGS
- [ ] IT LOOKED GOOD
- [ ] ONLY THING OPEN
- [ ] FORCED AGAINST WILL
- [ ] HUNGRY & DESPERATE
- [ ] WAS DRUNK

OTHER:

THE BEST THING(S) YOU ATE:

. . . .

THE WORST THING(S) YOU ATE:

. . . .

AMBIANCE
(1) (2) (3) (4) (5)

FOOD
(1) (2) (3) (4) (5)

SERVICE
(1) (2) (3) (4) (5)

THE ONE THING YOU'LL NEVER FORGET:

EAT HERE AGAIN? YES [ ] NO [ ] IF DESPERATE [ ]

A FEW MUST-TRYS

RESTAURANT	LOCATION
☐ MILKTOOTH	INDIANAPOLIS, IN
☐ LA SOMBRA DEL SABINO	TEPOZTLÁN, MEXICO
☐ MUCHACHO	ATLANTA, GA
☐ PALACE DINER	BIDDEFORD, ME
☐ HALF & HALF	ST. LOUIS, MO
☐ THE NASHVILLE BISCUIT HOUSE	NASHVILLE, TN
☐ SWEEDEEDEE	PORTLAND, OR
☐ PAPERBOY	AUSTIN, TX
☐ SUNNY POINTE CAFÉ	ASHEVILLE, NC
☐ THE FRONTIER RESTAURANT	ALBUQUERQUE, NM
☐ CRANKY AL'S	WAUWATOSA, WI
☐ POLLY'S PANCAKE PARLOR	SUGAR HILL, NH
☐ HELEN'S SAUSAGE HOUSE	SMYRNA, DE
☐ HAMBURG INN NO. 2	IOWA CITY, IA
☐ TIBBITTS AT FERN HILL	TACOMA, WA
☐ THE ORIGINAL PANTRY CAFÉ	LOS ANGELES, CA
☐ B&B SEI STELLE	SULMONA, ITALY
☐ VALENTINA'S TEX MEX BBQ	AUSTIN, TX
☐ KIHEI CAFFE	MAUI, HI
☐ THE JEFFERSON HOTEL	RICHMOND, VA
☐ PLOW	SAN FRANCISCO, CA
☐ RUSS & DAUGHTERS CAFE	NEW YORK, NY
☐ HAPPY GILLIS CAFE	KANSAS CITY, MO
☐ SABRINA'S CAFE	PHILADELPHIA, PA

WRITE-IN CANDIDATES

IN MORNING

AKA: BREAKFAST & BRUNCH

NAME OF THE RESTAURANT

NUMBER

022

PSST: ADD THIS TO THE INDEX(ES) IN THE BACK SO YOU CAN FIND IT QUICKLY LATER

WHERE WAS IT LOCATED?

CITY: STATE/COUNTRY:

WHY DID YOU EAT HERE?

☐ HEARD GREAT THINGS FORCED AGAINST WILL ☐

☐ IT LOOKED GOOD HUNGRY & DESPERATE ☐

☐ ONLY THING OPEN WAS DRUNK ☐

OTHER:

THE BEST THING(S) YOU ATE:

. . . .

AMBIANCE
① ② ③ ④ ⑤

FOOD
① ② ③ ④ ⑤

THE WORST THING(S) YOU ATE:

. . . .

SERVICE
① ② ③ ④ ⑤

THE ONE THING YOU'LL NEVER FORGET:

EAT HERE AGAIN? YES ☐ NO ☐ IF DESPERATE ☐

NUMBER   **NAME OF THE RESTAURANT**

023

PSST: ADD THIS TO THE INDEX(ES) IN THE BACK SO YOU CAN FIND IT QUICKLY LATER

WHERE WAS IT LOCATED?

CITY: STATE/COUNTRY:

WHY DID YOU EAT HERE?

☐ HEARD GREAT THINGS   FORCED AGAINST WILL ☐
☐ IT LOOKED GOOD   HUNGRY & DESPERATE ☐
☐ ONLY THING OPEN   WAS DRUNK ☐

OTHER:

AMBIANCE   THE BEST THING(S) YOU ATE:
① ② ③ ④ ⑤
. . . .
FOOD
① ② ③ ④ ⑤   THE WORST THING(S) YOU ATE:
SERVICE
① ② ③ ④ ⑤   . . . .

THE ONE THING YOU'LL NEVER FORGET:

EAT HERE AGAIN?   YES ☐   NO ☐   IF DESPERATE ☐

NAME OF THE RESTAURANT

NUMBER

024

PSST: ADD THIS TO THE INDEX(ES) IN THE BACK SO YOU CAN FIND IT QUICKLY LATER

WHERE WAS IT LOCATED?

CITY: STATE/COUNTRY:

WHY DID YOU EAT HERE?

- [ ] HEARD GREAT THINGS
- [ ] IT LOOKED GOOD
- [ ] ONLY THING OPEN
- [ ] FORCED AGAINST WILL
- [ ] HUNGRY & DESPERATE
- [ ] WAS DRUNK

OTHER:

THE BEST THING(S) YOU ATE:

. . . .

THE WORST THING(S) YOU ATE:

. . . .

AMBIANCE
(1) (2) (3) (4) (5)

FOOD
(1) (2) (3) (4) (5)

SERVICE
(1) (2) (3) (4) (5)

THE ONE THING YOU'LL NEVER FORGET:

EAT HERE AGAIN? YES [ ] NO [ ] IF DESPERATE [ ]

NUMBER

O25

NAME OF THE RESTAURANT

PSST: ADD THIS TO THE INDEX(ES) IN THE BACK SO YOU CAN FIND IT QUICKLY LATER

WHERE WAS IT LOCATED?

CITY: STATE/COUNTRY:

WHY DID YOU EAT HERE?

- [ ] HEARD GREAT THINGS
- [ ] IT LOOKED GOOD
- [ ] ONLY THING OPEN

- FORCED AGAINST WILL [ ]
- HUNGRY & DESPERATE [ ]
- WAS DRUNK [ ]

OTHER:

AMBIANCE
(1) (2) (3) (4) (5)

FOOD
(1) (2) (3) (4) (5)

SERVICE
(1) (2) (3) (4) (5)

THE BEST THING(S) YOU ATE:

. . . .

THE WORST THING(S) YOU ATE:

. . . .

THE ONE THING YOU'LL NEVER FORGET:

EAT HERE AGAIN?   YES [ ]   NO [ ]   IF DESPERATE [ ]

IN MORNING

AKA: BREAKFAST & BRUNCH

NAME OF THE RESTAURANT

NUMBER

026

PSST: ADD THIS TO THE INDEX(ES) IN THE BACK SO YOU CAN FIND IT QUICKLY LATER

WHERE WAS IT LOCATED?

CITY: STATE/COUNTRY:

WHY DID YOU EAT HERE?

☐ HEARD GREAT THINGS   FORCED AGAINST WILL ☐
☐ IT LOOKED GOOD   HUNGRY & DESPERATE ☐
☐ ONLY THING OPEN   WAS DRUNK ☐

OTHER:

THE BEST THING(S) YOU ATE:

. . . .

AMBIANCE
① ② ③ ④ ⑤

FOOD
① ② ③ ④ ⑤

THE WORST THING(S) YOU ATE:

. . . .

SERVICE
① ② ③ ④ ⑤

THE ONE THING YOU'LL NEVER FORGET:

EAT HERE AGAIN?   YES ☐   NO ☐   IF DESPERATE ☐

IN MORNING

NUMBER

027

NAME OF THE RESTAURANT

PSST: ADD THIS TO THE INDEX(ES) IN THE BACK SO YOU CAN FIND IT QUICKLY LATER

WHERE WAS IT LOCATED?

CITY: STATE/COUNTRY:

WHY DID YOU EAT HERE?

- [ ] HEARD GREAT THINGS
- [ ] IT LOOKED GOOD
- [ ] ONLY THING OPEN

- FORCED AGAINST WILL [ ]
- HUNGRY & DESPERATE [ ]
- WAS DRUNK [ ]

OTHER:

AMBIANCE
(1) (2) (3) (4) (5)

FOOD
(1) (2) (3) (4) (5)

SERVICE
(1) (2) (3) (4) (5)

THE BEST THING(S) YOU ATE:
. . . .

THE WORST THING(S) YOU ATE:
. . . .

THE ONE THING YOU'LL NEVER FORGET:

EAT HERE AGAIN?   YES [ ]   NO [ ]   IF DESPERATE [ ]

NAME OF THE RESTAURANT

NUMBER

028

PSST: ADD THIS TO THE INDEX(ES) IN THE BACK SO YOU CAN FIND IT QUICKLY LATER

WHERE WAS IT LOCATED?

CITY: STATE/COUNTRY:

WHY DID YOU EAT HERE?

☐ HEARD GREAT THINGS   FORCED AGAINST WILL ☐
☐ IT LOOKED GOOD   HUNGRY & DESPERATE ☐
☐ ONLY THING OPEN   WAS DRUNK ☐

OTHER:

THE BEST THING(S) YOU ATE:

. . . .

THE WORST THING(S) YOU ATE:

. . . .

AMBIANCE
① ② ③ ④ ⑤

FOOD
① ② ③ ④ ⑤

SERVICE
① ② ③ ④ ⑤

THE ONE THING YOU'LL NEVER FORGET:

EAT HERE AGAIN?   YES ☐   NO ☐   IF DESPERATE ☐

TAKE A FOOD TOUR

NEW ORLEANS, LA

RANKED THE BEST FOOD CITY IN AMERICA (2023)

LOCAL BREAKFAST SPECIALTIES

- [ ] EGGS SARDOU
- [ ] CHICORY COFFEE
- GRILLADES AND GRITS [ ]
- BEIGNETS [ ]

WAKING UP FOR BREAKFAST IN NEW ORLEANS MIGHT BE IMPOSSIBLE—BUT THAT'S WHY BRUNCH WAS INVENTED HERE IN 1854. SO NATURALLY, THERE IS NO SHORTAGE OF AMAZING 'MORNING-ISH' SPOTS TO EXPLORE.

RESTAURANT	KNOWN FOR
[ ] RUBY SLIPPER CAFE	ALL DAY BRUNCH
[ ] CAFÉ FLEUR DE LIS	CANDIED BACON
[ ] RUSSELL'S MARINA GRILL	ALLIGATOR SAUSAGE
[ ] ALMA CAFE	BUÑUELO MACHETEADAS
[ ] PAGODA CAFÉ	BREAKFAST TACOS
[ ] WAKIN' BAKIN'	QUESO BURRITO (W/ GRAVY)
[ ] STANLEY RESTAURANT	FRIED OYSTER BENEDICT
[ ] BISCUITS & BUNS ON BANKS	WAFFLEWICHES
[ ] WHO DAT COFFEE CAFE	CORN CAKES
[ ] BUTTERMILK DROP BAKERY	BUTTERMILK DROPS
[ ] ELIZABETH'S	BREAKFAST CALAS
[ ] NONNO'S CAJUN CUISINE	FRENCH TOAST
[ ] BRENNAN'S	BRANDY MILK PUNCH

WRITE-IN CANDIDATES

IN MORNING

AKA: BREAKFAST & BRUNCH

NAME OF THE RESTAURANT

NUMBER

029

PSST: ADD THIS TO THE INDEX(ES) IN THE BACK SO YOU CAN FIND IT QUICKLY LATER

WHERE WAS IT LOCATED?

CITY: STATE/COUNTRY:

WHY DID YOU EAT HERE?

- [ ] HEARD GREAT THINGS
- [ ] IT LOOKED GOOD
- [ ] ONLY THING OPEN
- [ ] FORCED AGAINST WILL
- [ ] HUNGRY & DESPERATE
- [ ] WAS DRUNK

OTHER:

THE BEST THING(S) YOU ATE:

. . . .

THE WORST THING(S) YOU ATE:

. . . .

AMBIANCE
① ② ③ ④ ⑤

FOOD
① ② ③ ④ ⑤

SERVICE
① ② ③ ④ ⑤

THE ONE THING YOU'LL NEVER FORGET:

EAT HERE AGAIN?   YES [ ]   NO [ ]   IF DESPERATE [ ]

NUMBER

030

NAME OF THE RESTAURANT

PSST: ADD THIS TO THE INDEX(ES) IN THE BACK SO YOU CAN FIND IT QUICKLY LATER

WHERE WAS IT LOCATED?

CITY: STATE/COUNTRY:

WHY DID YOU EAT HERE?

- [ ] HEARD GREAT THINGS
- [ ] IT LOOKED GOOD
- [ ] ONLY THING OPEN
- [ ] FORCED AGAINST WILL
- [ ] HUNGRY & DESPERATE
- [ ] WAS DRUNK

OTHER:

AMBIANCE
(1) (2) (3) (4) (5)

FOOD
(1) (2) (3) (4) (5)

SERVICE
(1) (2) (3) (4) (5)

THE BEST THING(S) YOU ATE:

. . . .

THE WORST THING(S) YOU ATE:

. . . .

THE ONE THING YOU'LL NEVER FORGET:

EAT HERE AGAIN?   YES [ ]   NO [ ]   IF DESPERATE [ ]

FROM THE STREETS

FROM THE STREETS

AKA: FOOD TRUCKS

NAME OF THE RESTAURANT

NUMBER

031

PSST: ADD THIS TO THE INDEX(ES) IN THE BACK SO YOU CAN FIND IT QUICKLY LATER

WHERE WAS IT LOCATED?

CITY: STATE/COUNTRY:

WHY DID YOU EAT HERE?

☐ HEARD GREAT THINGS   FORCED AGAINST WILL ☐

☐ IT LOOKED GOOD   HUNGRY & DESPERATE ☐

☐ ONLY THING OPEN   WAS DRUNK ☐

OTHER:

THE BEST THING(S) YOU ATE:

. . . .

THE WORST THING(S) YOU ATE:

. . . .

AMBIANCE
① ② ③ ④ ⑤

FOOD
① ② ③ ④ ⑤

SERVICE
① ② ③ ④ ⑤

THE ONE THING YOU'LL NEVER FORGET:

EAT HERE AGAIN?   YES ☐   NO ☐   IF DESPERATE ☐

FROM THE STREETS

NUMBER

032

NAME OF THE RESTAURANT

PSST: ADD THIS TO THE INDEX(ES) IN THE BACK SO YOU CAN FIND IT QUICKLY LATER

WHERE WAS IT LOCATED?

CITY: STATE/COUNTRY:

WHY DID YOU EAT HERE?

- [ ] HEARD GREAT THINGS
- [ ] IT LOOKED GOOD
- [ ] ONLY THING OPEN
- [ ] FORCED AGAINST WILL
- [ ] HUNGRY & DESPERATE
- [ ] WAS DRUNK

OTHER:

AMBIANCE
① ② ③ ④ ⑤

FOOD
① ② ③ ④ ⑤

SERVICE
① ② ③ ④ ⑤

THE BEST THING(S) YOU ATE:

· · · · · · · · · · · · · · · · · ·

THE WORST THING(S) YOU ATE:

· · · · · · · · · · · · · · · · · ·

THE ONE THING YOU'LL NEVER FORGET:

EAT HERE AGAIN?   YES [ ]   NO [ ]   IF DESPERATE [ ]

FROM THE STREETS

AKA: FOOD TRUCKS

NAME OF THE RESTAURANT

NUMBER

033

PSST: ADD THIS TO THE INDEX(ES) IN THE BACK SO YOU CAN FIND IT QUICKLY LATER

WHERE WAS IT LOCATED?

CITY: STATE/COUNTRY:

WHY DID YOU EAT HERE?

- [ ] HEARD GREAT THINGS
- [ ] IT LOOKED GOOD
- [ ] ONLY THING OPEN
- [ ] FORCED AGAINST WILL
- [ ] HUNGRY & DESPERATE
- [ ] WAS DRUNK

OTHER:

THE BEST THING(S) YOU ATE:

. . . .

THE WORST THING(S) YOU ATE:

. . . .

AMBIANCE
(1) (2) (3) (4) (5)

FOOD
(1) (2) (3) (4) (5)

SERVICE
(1) (2) (3) (4) (5)

THE ONE THING YOU'LL NEVER FORGET:

EAT HERE AGAIN?   YES [ ]   NO [ ]   IF DESPERATE [ ]

FROM THE STREETS

NUMBER

034

NAME OF THE RESTAURANT

PSST: ADD THIS TO THE INDEX(ES) IN THE BACK SO YOU CAN FIND IT QUICKLY LATER

WHERE WAS IT LOCATED?

CITY: STATE/COUNTRY:

WHY DID YOU EAT HERE?

☐ HEARD GREAT THINGS   FORCED AGAINST WILL ☐

☐ IT LOOKED GOOD   HUNGRY & DESPERATE ☐

☐ ONLY THING OPEN   WAS DRUNK ☐

OTHER:

AMBIANCE
① ② ③ ④ ⑤

FOOD
① ② ③ ④ ⑤

SERVICE
① ② ③ ④ ⑤

THE BEST THING(S) YOU ATE:

. . . .

THE WORST THING(S) YOU ATE:

. . . .

THE ONE THING YOU'LL NEVER FORGET:

EAT HERE AGAIN?   YES ☐   NO ☐   IF DESPERATE ☐

NAME OF THE RESTAURANT

NUMBER

035

PSST: ADD THIS TO THE INDEX(ES) IN THE BACK SO YOU CAN FIND IT QUICKLY LATER

WHERE WAS IT LOCATED?

CITY: STATE/COUNTRY:

WHY DID YOU EAT HERE?

☐ HEARD GREAT THINGS   FORCED AGAINST WILL ☐

☐ IT LOOKED GOOD   HUNGRY & DESPERATE ☐

☐ ONLY THING OPEN   WAS DRUNK ☐

OTHER:

THE BEST THING(S) YOU ATE:

. . . .

AMBIANCE
① ② ③ ④ ⑤

FOOD
① ② ③ ④ ⑤

THE WORST THING(S) YOU ATE:

. . . .

SERVICE
① ② ③ ④ ⑤

THE ONE THING YOU'LL NEVER FORGET:

EAT HERE AGAIN?   YES ☐   NO ☐   IF DESPERATE ☐

FROM THE STREETS

NUMBER

036

NAME OF THE RESTAURANT

PSST: ADD THIS TO THE INDEX(ES) IN THE BACK SO YOU CAN FIND IT QUICKLY LATER

WHERE WAS IT LOCATED?

CITY: STATE/COUNTRY:

WHY DID YOU EAT HERE?

☐ HEARD GREAT THINGS   FORCED AGAINST WILL ☐

☐ IT LOOKED GOOD   HUNGRY & DESPERATE ☐

☐ ONLY THING OPEN   WAS DRUNK ☐

OTHER:

AMBIANCE

① ② ③ ④ ⑤

THE BEST THING(S) YOU ATE:

. . . .

FOOD

① ② ③ ④ ⑤

THE WORST THING(S) YOU ATE:

SERVICE

① ② ③ ④ ⑤

. . . .

THE ONE THING YOU'LL NEVER FORGET:

EAT HERE AGAIN?   YES ☐   NO ☐   IF DESPERATE ☐

NAME OF THE RESTAURANT

NUMBER

037

PSST: ADD THIS TO THE INDEX(ES) IN THE BACK SO YOU CAN FIND IT QUICKLY LATER

WHERE WAS IT LOCATED?

CITY: STATE/COUNTRY:

WHY DID YOU EAT HERE?

- [ ] HEARD GREAT THINGS
- [ ] IT LOOKED GOOD
- [ ] ONLY THING OPEN
- [ ] FORCED AGAINST WILL
- [ ] HUNGRY & DESPERATE
- [ ] WAS DRUNK

OTHER:

THE BEST THING(S) YOU ATE:

. . . .

AMBIANCE
① ② ③ ④ ⑤

FOOD
① ② ③ ④ ⑤

THE WORST THING(S) YOU ATE:

. . . .

SERVICE
① ② ③ ④ ⑤

THE ONE THING YOU'LL NEVER FORGET:

EAT HERE AGAIN?   YES [ ]   NO [ ]   IF DESPERATE [ ]

OUR FAVORITES

☐ **BEEN THERE**   ## I DREAM OF WEENIE

113 S 11TH ST, NASHVILLE, TN 37206

A FEW FAVORITES

☐ MAC AND CHEESE WEENIE

☐ PIMENTO CHEESE WEENIE

☐ THE REBEL YELP

USE OF 'WEENIE'
① ② ③ ④ ⑤

SEXY HOT DOG LOGO
① ② ③ ④ ⑤

SURE, THIS PLACE PROBABLY GETS A LOT OF ATTENTION FOR THE FACT THAT THE 'WEENIES' ARE SERVED OUT OF A CONVERTED VW BUS—BUT THAT'S NOT WHY WE LOVE IT. WE CAN SUM IT UP IN TWO WORDS: HOT DOGS. IF YOU KNOW US, IT'S NO SECRET THAT WE LOVE THEM—AND THIS PLACE MAKES SOME OF THE BEST WE'VE EVER HAD. IN OUR OPINION, THE MAC AND CHEESE 'WEENIE' IS THE MUST HAVE ITEM ON THE MENU—BUT FEEL FREE TO CALL IT A HOT DOG. WE DO.

☐ **BEEN THERE**   ## TACO REPUBLIC

SERVICES THE KANSAS CITY METRO AREA

A FEW FAVORITES

☐ OLD SCHOOL STREET TACO

☐ TECATE BARBACOA STREET TACO

☐ QUESO JOSÉ

DELICIOUSNESS
① ② ③ ④ ⑤

GREASINESS
① ② ③ ④ ⑤

WHILE THEY HAVE A BRICK & MORTAR LOCATION NOW, THERE IS JUST SOMETHING BETTER ABOUT GETTING THE TACOS STRAIGHT FROM THE ORIGINAL TRUCK THEY GOT STARTED IN. HONESTLY, WE USED TO STALK THIS TRUCK AROUND TOWN WHEN THEY FIRST OPENED UP—THEY ARE JUST THAT GOOD. I'M NOT TOO PROUD TO ADMIT THAT I ONCE ATE SEVEN OF THEIR BARBACOA TACOS IN ONE SITTING. THAT'S EITHER A TESTAMENT TO THEIR TACOS OR A STATEMENT ABOUT ME—OR PROBABLY BOTH.

FROM THE STREETS

AKA: FOOD TRUCKS

NAME OF THE RESTAURANT

NUMBER

038

PSST: ADD THIS TO THE INDEX(ES) IN THE BACK SO YOU CAN FIND IT QUICKLY LATER

WHERE WAS IT LOCATED?

CITY: STATE/COUNTRY:

WHY DID YOU EAT HERE?

☐ HEARD GREAT THINGS   FORCED AGAINST WILL ☐

☐ IT LOOKED GOOD   HUNGRY & DESPERATE ☐

☐ ONLY THING OPEN   WAS DRUNK ☐

OTHER:

THE BEST THING(S) YOU ATE:

. . . .

AMBIANCE
① ② ③ ④ ⑤

FOOD
① ② ③ ④ ⑤

THE WORST THING(S) YOU ATE:

. . . .

SERVICE
① ② ③ ④ ⑤

THE ONE THING YOU'LL NEVER FORGET:

EAT HERE AGAIN?   YES ☐   NO ☐   IF DESPERATE ☐

NUMBER

039

NAME OF THE RESTAURANT

PSST: ADD THIS TO THE INDEX(ES) IN THE BACK SO YOU CAN FIND IT QUICKLY LATER

WHERE WAS IT LOCATED?

CITY: STATE/COUNTRY:

WHY DID YOU EAT HERE?

☐ HEARD GREAT THINGS   FORCED AGAINST WILL ☐

☐ IT LOOKED GOOD   HUNGRY & DESPERATE ☐

☐ ONLY THING OPEN   WAS DRUNK ☐

OTHER:

AMBIANCE

① ② ③ ④ ⑤

FOOD

① ② ③ ④ ⑤

SERVICE

① ② ③ ④ ⑤

THE BEST THING(S) YOU ATE:

. . . .

THE WORST THING(S) YOU ATE:

. . . .

THE ONE THING YOU'LL NEVER FORGET:

EAT HERE AGAIN?   YES ☐   NO ☐   IF DESPERATE ☐

FROM THE STREETS

AKA: FOOD TRUCKS

NAME OF THE RESTAURANT

NUMBER

040

PSST: ADD THIS TO THE INDEX(ES) IN THE BACK SO YOU CAN FIND IT QUICKLY LATER

WHERE WAS IT LOCATED?

CITY: STATE/COUNTRY:

WHY DID YOU EAT HERE?

- [ ] HEARD GREAT THINGS
- [ ] IT LOOKED GOOD
- [ ] ONLY THING OPEN

- FORCED AGAINST WILL [ ]
- HUNGRY & DESPERATE [ ]
- WAS DRUNK [ ]

OTHER:

THE BEST THING(S) YOU ATE:

. . . .

THE WORST THING(S) YOU ATE:

. . . .

AMBIANCE
① ② ③ ④ ⑤

FOOD
① ② ③ ④ ⑤

SERVICE
① ② ③ ④ ⑤

THE ONE THING YOU'LL NEVER FORGET:

EAT HERE AGAIN?   YES [ ]   NO [ ]   IF DESPERATE [ ]

NUMBER

041

NAME OF THE RESTAURANT

PSST: ADD THIS TO THE INDEX(ES) IN THE BACK SO YOU CAN FIND IT QUICKLY LATER

WHERE WAS IT LOCATED?

CITY: STATE/COUNTRY:

WHY DID YOU EAT HERE?

☐ HEARD GREAT THINGS FORCED AGAINST WILL ☐

☐ IT LOOKED GOOD HUNGRY & DESPERATE ☐

☐ ONLY THING OPEN WAS DRUNK ☐

OTHER:

AMBIANCE

① ② ③ ④ ⑤

FOOD

① ② ③ ④ ⑤

SERVICE

① ② ③ ④ ⑤

THE BEST THING(S) YOU ATE:

. . . .

THE WORST THING(S) YOU ATE:

. . . .

THE ONE THING YOU'LL NEVER FORGET:

EAT HERE AGAIN? YES ☐ NO ☐ IF DESPERATE ☐

FROM THE STREETS

AKA: FOOD TRUCKS

NAME OF THE RESTAURANT

NUMBER

042

PSST: ADD THIS TO THE INDEX(ES) IN THE BACK SO YOU CAN FIND IT QUICKLY LATER

WHERE WAS IT LOCATED?

CITY: STATE/COUNTRY:

WHY DID YOU EAT HERE?

☐ HEARD GREAT THINGS
☐ IT LOOKED GOOD
☐ ONLY THING OPEN

FORCED AGAINST WILL ☐
HUNGRY & DESPERATE ☐
WAS DRUNK ☐

OTHER:

THE BEST THING(S) YOU ATE:

. . . .

THE WORST THING(S) YOU ATE:

. . . .

AMBIANCE
① ② ③ ④ ⑤

FOOD
① ② ③ ④ ⑤

SERVICE
① ② ③ ④ ⑤

THE ONE THING YOU'LL NEVER FORGET:

EAT HERE AGAIN? YES ☐ NO ☐ IF DESPERATE ☐

NUMBER

043

NAME OF THE RESTAURANT

PSST: ADD THIS TO THE INDEX(ES) IN THE BACK SO YOU CAN FIND IT QUICKLY LATER

WHERE WAS IT LOCATED?

CITY: STATE/COUNTRY:

WHY DID YOU EAT HERE?

- [ ] HEARD GREAT THINGS
- [ ] IT LOOKED GOOD
- [ ] ONLY THING OPEN

- FORCED AGAINST WILL [ ]
- HUNGRY & DESPERATE [ ]
- WAS DRUNK [ ]

OTHER:

AMBIANCE
(1) (2) (3) (4) (5)

FOOD
(1) (2) (3) (4) (5)

SERVICE
(1) (2) (3) (4) (5)

THE BEST THING(S) YOU ATE:

. . . .

THE WORST THING(S) YOU ATE:

. . . .

THE ONE THING YOU'LL NEVER FORGET:

EAT HERE AGAIN?   YES [ ]   NO [ ]   IF DESPERATE [ ]

FROM THE STREETS

AKA: FOOD TRUCKS

NAME OF THE RESTAURANT

NUMBER

044

PSST: ADD THIS TO THE INDEX(ES) IN THE BACK SO YOU CAN FIND IT QUICKLY LATER

WHERE WAS IT LOCATED?

CITY: STATE/COUNTRY:

WHY DID YOU EAT HERE?

- [ ] HEARD GREAT THINGS
- [ ] IT LOOKED GOOD
- [ ] ONLY THING OPEN
- [ ] FORCED AGAINST WILL
- [ ] HUNGRY & DESPERATE
- [ ] WAS DRUNK

OTHER:

THE BEST THING(S) YOU ATE:

. . . .

AMBIANCE
① ② ③ ④ ⑤

FOOD
① ② ③ ④ ⑤

THE WORST THING(S) YOU ATE:

. . . .

SERVICE
① ② ③ ④ ⑤

THE ONE THING YOU'LL NEVER FORGET:

EAT HERE AGAIN?   YES [ ]   NO [ ]   IF DESPERATE [ ]

STREET TACOS

NATIONAL TACO DAY IS ON OCTOBER 4TH

PERFECT FOR	TERRIBLE FOR
☐ TUESDAYS	RUINING CLOTHES ☐
☐ ALL OTHER DAYS	RUINING DIETS ☐

THE TERM 'TACO' WAS FIRST USED BY MEXICAN SILVER MINERS IN THE 1700s TO REFER TO THE PAPER WRAPPED GUNPOWDER THAT THEY WOULD WEDGE INTO CRACKS IN ROCK IN ORDER TO MINE. EVENTUALLY THE WORKERS STARTED TO CALL THEIR TORTILLA-WRAPPED LUNCHES 'TACOS' DUE TO A RESEMBLANCE TO THE EXPLOSIVES.

FIND NOTABLES AT: **LOCATION**

☐ CARNITAS URUAPAN		CHICAGO, IL
☐ CUCINA ZAPATA		PHILADELPHIA, PA
☐ BIRRIA-LANDIA		NEW YORK, NY
☐ SMOKE ET AL		NASHVILLE, TN
☐ TACOS TIERRA CALIENTE		HOUSTON, TX
☐ LEO'S TACOS TRUCK		LOS ANGELES, CA
☐ TAQUERIA SINALOA		OAKLAND, CA
☐ SEOUL TACO		ST. LOUIS, MO
☐ YUMBII		ATLANTA, GA
☐ AZTEC DAVE'S		CHICAGO, IL
☐ PEACHED TORTILLA		AUSTIN, TX
☐ KOGI BBQ TACO TRUCK		LOS ANGELES, CA

WRITE-IN CANDIDATES

FROM THE STREETS

AKA: FOOD TRUCKS

NAME OF THE RESTAURANT

NUMBER

045

PSST: ADD THIS TO THE INDEX(ES) IN THE BACK SO YOU CAN FIND IT QUICKLY LATER

WHERE WAS IT LOCATED?

CITY: STATE/COUNTRY:

WHY DID YOU EAT HERE?

- [ ] HEARD GREAT THINGS
- [ ] IT LOOKED GOOD
- [ ] ONLY THING OPEN
- [ ] FORCED AGAINST WILL
- [ ] HUNGRY & DESPERATE
- [ ] WAS DRUNK

OTHER:

THE BEST THING(S) YOU ATE:

. . . .

THE WORST THING(S) YOU ATE:

. . . .

AMBIANCE
① ② ③ ④ ⑤

FOOD
① ② ③ ④ ⑤

SERVICE
① ② ③ ④ ⑤

THE ONE THING YOU'LL NEVER FORGET:

EAT HERE AGAIN? YES [ ] NO [ ] IF DESPERATE [ ]

NUMBER

046

NAME OF THE RESTAURANT

PSST: ADD THIS TO THE INDEX(ES) IN THE BACK SO YOU CAN FIND IT QUICKLY LATER

WHERE WAS IT LOCATED?

CITY: STATE/COUNTRY:

WHY DID YOU EAT HERE?

☐ HEARD GREAT THINGS   FORCED AGAINST WILL ☐

☐ IT LOOKED GOOD   HUNGRY & DESPERATE ☐

☐ ONLY THING OPEN   WAS DRUNK ☐

OTHER:

AMBIANCE
① ② ③ ④ ⑤

FOOD
① ② ③ ④ ⑤

SERVICE
① ② ③ ④ ⑤

THE BEST THING(S) YOU ATE:

. . . .

THE WORST THING(S) YOU ATE:

. . . .

THE ONE THING YOU'LL NEVER FORGET:

EAT HERE AGAIN?   YES ☐   NO ☐   IF DESPERATE ☐

NAME OF THE RESTAURANT

NUMBER

047

PSST: ADD THIS TO THE INDEX(ES) IN THE BACK SO YOU CAN FIND IT QUICKLY LATER

WHERE WAS IT LOCATED?

CITY: STATE/COUNTRY:

WHY DID YOU EAT HERE?

- [ ] HEARD GREAT THINGS
- [ ] IT LOOKED GOOD
- [ ] ONLY THING OPEN
- [ ] FORCED AGAINST WILL
- [ ] HUNGRY & DESPERATE
- [ ] WAS DRUNK

OTHER:

THE BEST THING(S) YOU ATE:

. . . .

THE WORST THING(S) YOU ATE:

. . . .

AMBIANCE
(1) (2) (3) (4) (5)

FOOD
(1) (2) (3) (4) (5)

SERVICE
(1) (2) (3) (4) (5)

THE ONE THING YOU'LL NEVER FORGET:

EAT HERE AGAIN?   YES [ ]   NO [ ]   IF DESPERATE [ ]

FROM THE STREETS

NUMBER

048

NAME OF THE RESTAURANT

PSST: ADD THIS TO THE INDEX(ES) IN THE BACK SO YOU CAN FIND IT QUICKLY LATER

WHERE WAS IT LOCATED?

CITY: STATE/COUNTRY:

WHY DID YOU EAT HERE?

- [ ] HEARD GREAT THINGS
- [ ] IT LOOKED GOOD
- [ ] ONLY THING OPEN
- [ ] FORCED AGAINST WILL
- [ ] HUNGRY & DESPERATE
- [ ] WAS DRUNK

OTHER:

AMBIANCE
(1) (2) (3) (4) (5)

FOOD
(1) (2) (3) (4) (5)

SERVICE
(1) (2) (3) (4) (5)

THE BEST THING(S) YOU ATE:

. . . .

THE WORST THING(S) YOU ATE:

. . . .

THE ONE THING YOU'LL NEVER FORGET:

EAT HERE AGAIN?   YES [ ]   NO [ ]   IF DESPERATE [ ]

FROM THE STREETS

AKA: FOOD TRUCKS

NAME OF THE RESTAURANT

NUMBER

049

PSST: ADD THIS TO THE INDEX(ES) IN THE BACK SO YOU CAN FIND IT QUICKLY LATER

WHERE WAS IT LOCATED?

CITY: STATE/COUNTRY:

WHY DID YOU EAT HERE?

- [ ] HEARD GREAT THINGS
- [ ] IT LOOKED GOOD
- [ ] ONLY THING OPEN

- FORCED AGAINST WILL [ ]
- HUNGRY & DESPERATE [ ]
- WAS DRUNK [ ]

OTHER:

THE BEST THING(S) YOU ATE:

. . . .

THE WORST THING(S) YOU ATE:

. . . .

AMBIANCE
(1) (2) (3) (4) (5)

FOOD
(1) (2) (3) (4) (5)

SERVICE
(1) (2) (3) (4) (5)

THE ONE THING YOU'LL NEVER FORGET:

EAT HERE AGAIN?   YES [ ]   NO [ ]   IF DESPERATE [ ]

FROM THE STREETS

NUMBER

050

NAME OF THE RESTAURANT

PSST: ADD THIS TO THE INDEX(ES) IN THE BACK SO YOU CAN FIND IT QUICKLY LATER

WHERE WAS IT LOCATED?

CITY: STATE/COUNTRY:

WHY DID YOU EAT HERE?

- [ ] HEARD GREAT THINGS
- [ ] IT LOOKED GOOD
- [ ] ONLY THING OPEN
- [ ] FORCED AGAINST WILL
- [ ] HUNGRY & DESPERATE
- [ ] WAS DRUNK

OTHER:

AMBIANCE
① ② ③ ④ ⑤

FOOD
① ② ③ ④ ⑤

SERVICE
① ② ③ ④ ⑤

THE BEST THING(S) YOU ATE:

. . . .

THE WORST THING(S) YOU ATE:

. . . .

THE ONE THING YOU'LL NEVER FORGET:

EAT HERE AGAIN?   YES [ ]   NO [ ]   IF DESPERATE [ ]

NAME OF THE RESTAURANT

NUMBER

O51

PSST: ADD THIS TO THE INDEX(ES) IN THE BACK SO YOU CAN FIND IT QUICKLY LATER

WHERE WAS IT LOCATED?

CITY: STATE/COUNTRY:

WHY DID YOU EAT HERE?

☐ HEARD GREAT THINGS FORCED AGAINST WILL ☐

☐ IT LOOKED GOOD HUNGRY & DESPERATE ☐

☐ ONLY THING OPEN WAS DRUNK ☐

OTHER:

THE BEST THING(S) YOU ATE:

. . . .

THE WORST THING(S) YOU ATE:

. . . .

AMBIANCE
① ② ③ ④ ⑤

FOOD
① ② ③ ④ ⑤

SERVICE
① ② ③ ④ ⑤

THE ONE THING YOU'LL NEVER FORGET:

EAT HERE AGAIN? YES ☐ NO ☐ IF DESPERATE ☐

RESTAURANT	LOCATION
☐ MS. CHEEZIOUS	MIAMI, FL
☐ BANG BITE FILLING STATION	SANTA FE, NM
☐ NONG'S KHAO MAN GAI	PORTLAND, OR
☐ LE CAMION QUI FUME	PARIS, FRANCE
☐ THE LOBOS TRUCK	LOS ANGELES, CA
☐ DANGER DOGS	MELBOURNE, AUSTRALIA
☐ DIE DOLLEN KNOLLEN	BERLIN, GERMANY
☐ HURT'S HOT CHICKEN	NASHVILLE, TN
☐ ROTI ROLLS	CHARLESTON, SC
☐ MICKLETHWAIT CRAFT MEATS	AUSTIN, TX
☐ STREETZA PIZZA	MILWAUKEE, WI
☐ THE DUCK TRUCK	MONTREAL, CANADA
☐ BIG WAVE SHRIMP	HALEIWA, HI
☐ GASTROS	PROVIDENCE, RI
☐ TOT BOSS	ST. PAUL, MN
☐ EMERSON FRY BREAD	PHOENIX, AZ
☐ MANNINO'S CANNOLI EXPRESS	HAMMONTON, NJ
☐ CHURROS BROS	LONDON, ENGLAND
☐ HERO OR VILLAIN	DETROIT, MI
☐ BLAXICAN SOUL FOOD	ATLANTA, GA
☐ YETI DOGS	ANCHORAGE, AK
☐ PHO NOMENAL DUMPLINGS	RALEIGH, NC
☐ GASTROS	PROVIDENCE, RI
☐ FLASH CRABCAKE	BALTIMORE, MD

WRITE-IN CANDIDATES

FROM THE STREETS

AKA: FOOD TRUCKS

NAME OF THE RESTAURANT

NUMBER

052

PSST: ADD THIS TO THE INDEX(ES) IN THE BACK SO YOU CAN FIND IT QUICKLY LATER

WHERE WAS IT LOCATED?

CITY: STATE/COUNTRY:

WHY DID YOU EAT HERE?

- [ ] HEARD GREAT THINGS
- [ ] IT LOOKED GOOD
- [ ] ONLY THING OPEN
- [ ] FORCED AGAINST WILL
- [ ] HUNGRY & DESPERATE
- [ ] WAS DRUNK

OTHER:

THE BEST THING(S) YOU ATE:

. . . .

THE WORST THING(S) YOU ATE:

. . . .

AMBIANCE
① ② ③ ④ ⑤

FOOD
① ② ③ ④ ⑤

SERVICE
① ② ③ ④ ⑤

THE ONE THING YOU'LL NEVER FORGET:

EAT HERE AGAIN?   YES [ ]   NO [ ]   IF DESPERATE [ ]

FROM THE STREETS

NUMBER

053

NAME OF THE RESTAURANT

PSST: ADD THIS TO THE INDEX(ES) IN THE BACK SO YOU CAN FIND IT QUICKLY LATER

WHERE WAS IT LOCATED?

CITY: STATE/COUNTRY:

WHY DID YOU EAT HERE?

- [ ] HEARD GREAT THINGS
- [ ] IT LOOKED GOOD
- [ ] ONLY THING OPEN
- [ ] FORCED AGAINST WILL
- [ ] HUNGRY & DESPERATE
- [ ] WAS DRUNK

OTHER:

AMBIANCE
(1) (2) (3) (4) (5)

FOOD
(1) (2) (3) (4) (5)

SERVICE
(1) (2) (3) (4) (5)

THE BEST THING(S) YOU ATE:
. . . .

THE WORST THING(S) YOU ATE:
. . . .

THE ONE THING YOU'LL NEVER FORGET:

EAT HERE AGAIN?   YES [ ]   NO [ ]   IF DESPERATE [ ]

FROM THE STREETS

NAME OF THE RESTAURANT

NUMBER

054

PSST: ADD THIS TO THE INDEX(ES) IN THE BACK SO YOU CAN FIND IT QUICKLY LATER

WHERE WAS IT LOCATED?

CITY: STATE/COUNTRY:

WHY DID YOU EAT HERE?

- [ ] HEARD GREAT THINGS
- [ ] IT LOOKED GOOD
- [ ] ONLY THING OPEN
- [ ] FORCED AGAINST WILL
- [ ] HUNGRY & DESPERATE
- [ ] WAS DRUNK

OTHER:

THE BEST THING(S) YOU ATE:

. . . .

THE WORST THING(S) YOU ATE:

. . . .

AMBIANCE
① ② ③ ④ ⑤

FOOD
① ② ③ ④ ⑤

SERVICE
① ② ③ ④ ⑤

THE ONE THING YOU'LL NEVER FORGET:

EAT HERE AGAIN?   YES [ ]   NO [ ]   IF DESPERATE [ ]

FROM THE STREETS

NUMBER

055

NAME OF THE RESTAURANT

PSST: ADD THIS TO THE INDEX(ES) IN THE BACK SO YOU CAN FIND IT QUICKLY LATER

WHERE WAS IT LOCATED?

CITY: STATE/COUNTRY:

WHY DID YOU EAT HERE?

- [ ] HEARD GREAT THINGS
- [ ] IT LOOKED GOOD
- [ ] ONLY THING OPEN
- [ ] FORCED AGAINST WILL
- [ ] HUNGRY & DESPERATE
- [ ] WAS DRUNK

OTHER:

AMBIANCE
① ② ③ ④ ⑤

FOOD
① ② ③ ④ ⑤

SERVICE
① ② ③ ④ ⑤

THE BEST THING(S) YOU ATE:

. . . .

THE WORST THING(S) YOU ATE:

. . . .

THE ONE THING YOU'LL NEVER FORGET:

EAT HERE AGAIN?   YES [ ]   NO [ ]   IF DESPERATE [ ]

NAME OF THE RESTAURANT

NUMBER

056

PSST: ADD THIS TO THE INDEX(ES) IN THE BACK SO YOU CAN FIND IT QUICKLY LATER

WHERE WAS IT LOCATED?

CITY: STATE/COUNTRY:

WHY DID YOU EAT HERE?

☐ HEARD GREAT THINGS   FORCED AGAINST WILL ☐

☐ IT LOOKED GOOD   HUNGRY & DESPERATE ☐

☐ ONLY THING OPEN   WAS DRUNK ☐

OTHER:

THE BEST THING(S) YOU ATE:

. . . .

AMBIANCE
① ② ③ ④ ⑤

FOOD
① ② ③ ④ ⑤

THE WORST THING(S) YOU ATE:

. . . .

SERVICE
① ② ③ ④ ⑤

THE ONE THING YOU'LL NEVER FORGET:

EAT HERE AGAIN?   YES ☐   NO ☐   IF DESPERATE ☐

NUMBER

057

NAME OF THE RESTAURANT

PSST: ADD THIS TO THE INDEX(ES) IN THE BACK SO YOU CAN FIND IT QUICKLY LATER

WHERE WAS IT LOCATED?

CITY: STATE/COUNTRY:

WHY DID YOU EAT HERE?

- [ ] HEARD GREAT THINGS
- [ ] IT LOOKED GOOD
- [ ] ONLY THING OPEN

- [ ] FORCED AGAINST WILL
- [ ] HUNGRY & DESPERATE
- [ ] WAS DRUNK

OTHER:

AMBIANCE
(1) (2) (3) (4) (5)

FOOD
(1) (2) (3) (4) (5)

SERVICE
(1) (2) (3) (4) (5)

THE BEST THING(S) YOU ATE:

. . . .

THE WORST THING(S) YOU ATE:

. . . .

THE ONE THING YOU'LL NEVER FORGET:

EAT HERE AGAIN?   YES [ ]   NO [ ]   IF DESPERATE [ ]

FROM THE STREETS

AKA: FOOD TRUCKS

NAME OF THE RESTAURANT

NUMBER

O58

PSST: ADD THIS TO THE INDEX(ES) IN THE BACK SO YOU CAN FIND IT QUICKLY LATER

WHERE WAS IT LOCATED?

CITY: STATE/COUNTRY:

WHY DID YOU EAT HERE?

☐ HEARD GREAT THINGS   FORCED AGAINST WILL ☐

☐ IT LOOKED GOOD   HUNGRY & DESPERATE ☐

☐ ONLY THING OPEN   WAS DRUNK ☐

OTHER:

THE BEST THING(S) YOU ATE:

. . . .

THE WORST THING(S) YOU ATE:

. . . .

AMBIANCE

① ② ③ ④ ⑤

FOOD

① ② ③ ④ ⑤

SERVICE

① ② ③ ④ ⑤

THE ONE THING YOU'LL NEVER FORGET:

EAT HERE AGAIN?   YES ☐   NO ☐   IF DESPERATE ☐

TAKE A FOOD TOUR

PORTLAND, OR

TECHNICALLY THEY'RE CALLED FOOD CARTS HERE

NOTABLE FOOD CART 'DISTRICTS'

- [ ] PROST MARKETPLACE
- [ ] FRENCH QUARTER
- [ ] CARTOPIA FOOD CARTS
- [ ] HINTERLAND BAR

THANKS TO RELATIVELY LOW-REGULATION COMPARED TO OTHER U.S. CITIES, PORTLAND IS HOME TO OVER 600 FOOD CARTS CITY-WIDE. DON'T WORRY THOUGH, FOOD SAFETY IS STILL STRICTLY ENFORCED.

RESTAURANT	KNOWN FOR
[ ] KEE'S LOADED KITCHEN	MAC & CHEESE
[ ] BAON KAINAN	CHICKEN ADOBO
[ ] MOLE MOLE MEXICAN CUISINE	MOLES
[ ] ERICA'S SOUL FOOD	CHICKEN WINGS
[ ] YOSHI'S SUSHI	SUSHI ROLLS
[ ] BAKE ON THE RUN	GUYANESE CUISINE
[ ] TITO'S TAQUITOS	TAQUITOS
[ ] BING MI	JIANBING
[ ] STRETCH THE NOODLE	HAND-PULLED NOODLES
[ ] DESI PDX	INDIAN CUISINE
[ ] MATTA	VIETNAMESE-AMERICAN
[ ] FARMER AND THE BEAST	SMASH BURGERS
[ ] MATT'S BBQ	BRISKET

WRITE-IN CANDIDATES

FROM THE STREETS

AKA: FOOD TRUCKS

NAME OF THE RESTAURANT

NUMBER

059

PSST: ADD THIS TO THE INDEX(ES) IN THE BACK SO YOU CAN FIND IT QUICKLY LATER

WHERE WAS IT LOCATED?

CITY: STATE/COUNTRY:

WHY DID YOU EAT HERE?

☐ HEARD GREAT THINGS   FORCED AGAINST WILL ☐

☐ IT LOOKED GOOD   HUNGRY & DESPERATE ☐

☐ ONLY THING OPEN   WAS DRUNK ☐

OTHER:

THE BEST THING(S) YOU ATE:

. . . .

THE WORST THING(S) YOU ATE:

. . . .

AMBIANCE
① ② ③ ④ ⑤

FOOD
① ② ③ ④ ⑤

SERVICE
① ② ③ ④ ⑤

THE ONE THING YOU'LL NEVER FORGET:

EAT HERE AGAIN?   YES ☐   NO ☐   IF DESPERATE ☐

FROM THE STREETS

NUMBER

060

NAME OF THE RESTAURANT

PSST: ADD THIS TO THE INDEX(ES) IN THE BACK SO YOU CAN FIND IT QUICKLY LATER

WHERE WAS IT LOCATED?

CITY: STATE/COUNTRY:

WHY DID YOU EAT HERE?

- [ ] HEARD GREAT THINGS
- [ ] IT LOOKED GOOD
- [ ] ONLY THING OPEN
- [ ] FORCED AGAINST WILL
- [ ] HUNGRY & DESPERATE
- [ ] WAS DRUNK

OTHER:

AMBIANCE
(1) (2) (3) (4) (5)

FOOD
(1) (2) (3) (4) (5)

SERVICE
(1) (2) (3) (4) (5)

THE BEST THING(S) YOU ATE:

. . . .

THE WORST THING(S) YOU ATE:

. . . .

THE ONE THING YOU'LL NEVER FORGET:

EAT HERE AGAIN?   YES [ ]   NO [ ]   IF DESPERATE [ ]

HOLE IN THE WALLS

HOLE IN THE WALLS
AKA: DIVES & DINERS

NAME OF THE RESTAURANT

NUMBER

061

PSST: ADD THIS TO THE INDEX(ES) IN THE BACK SO YOU CAN FIND IT QUICKLY LATER

WHERE WAS IT LOCATED?

CITY: STATE/COUNTRY:

WHY DID YOU EAT HERE?

- [ ] HEARD GREAT THINGS
- [ ] IT LOOKED GOOD
- [ ] ONLY THING OPEN
- [ ] FORCED AGAINST WILL
- [ ] HUNGRY & DESPERATE
- [ ] WAS DRUNK

OTHER:

THE BEST THING(S) YOU ATE:

. . . .

AMBIANCE
(1) (2) (3) (4) (5)

FOOD
(1) (2) (3) (4) (5)

THE WORST THING(S) YOU ATE:

. . . .

SERVICE
(1) (2) (3) (4) (5)

THE ONE THING YOU'LL NEVER FORGET:

EAT HERE AGAIN?   YES [ ]   NO [ ]   IF DESPERATE [ ]

NUMBER

062

PSST: ADD THIS TO THE INDEX(ES) IN THE BACK SO YOU CAN FIND IT QUICKLY LATER

NAME OF THE RESTAURANT

WHERE WAS IT LOCATED?

CITY: STATE/COUNTRY:

WHY DID YOU EAT HERE?

☐ HEARD GREAT THINGS   FORCED AGAINST WILL ☐
☐ IT LOOKED GOOD   HUNGRY & DESPERATE ☐
☐ ONLY THING OPEN   WAS DRUNK ☐

OTHER:

AMBIANCE
① ② ③ ④ ⑤

FOOD
① ② ③ ④ ⑤

SERVICE
① ② ③ ④ ⑤

THE BEST THING(S) YOU ATE:
. . . .

THE WORST THING(S) YOU ATE:
. . . .

THE ONE THING YOU'LL NEVER FORGET:

EAT HERE AGAIN?   YES ☐   NO ☐   IF DESPERATE ☐

HOLE IN THE WALLS AKA: DIVES & DINERS

NAME OF THE RESTAURANT

NUMBER

063

PSST: ADD THIS TO THE INDEX(ES) IN THE BACK SO YOU CAN FIND IT QUICKLY LATER

WHERE WAS IT LOCATED?

CITY: STATE/COUNTRY:

WHY DID YOU EAT HERE?

- [ ] HEARD GREAT THINGS
- [ ] IT LOOKED GOOD
- [ ] ONLY THING OPEN
- [ ] FORCED AGAINST WILL
- [ ] HUNGRY & DESPERATE
- [ ] WAS DRUNK

OTHER:

THE BEST THING(S) YOU ATE:

. . . .

THE WORST THING(S) YOU ATE:

. . . .

AMBIANCE
① ② ③ ④ ⑤

FOOD
① ② ③ ④ ⑤

SERVICE
① ② ③ ④ ⑤

THE ONE THING YOU'LL NEVER FORGET:

EAT HERE AGAIN?   YES [ ]   NO [ ]   IF DESPERATE [ ]

NUMBER

064

NAME OF THE RESTAURANT

PSST: ADD THIS TO THE INDEX(ES) IN THE BACK SO YOU CAN FIND IT QUICKLY LATER

WHERE WAS IT LOCATED?

CITY: STATE/COUNTRY:

WHY DID YOU EAT HERE?

☐ HEARD GREAT THINGS   FORCED AGAINST WILL ☐

☐ IT LOOKED GOOD   HUNGRY & DESPERATE ☐

☐ ONLY THING OPEN   WAS DRUNK ☐

OTHER:

AMBIANCE

① ② ③ ④ ⑤

THE BEST THING(S) YOU ATE:

. . . .

FOOD

① ② ③ ④ ⑤

THE WORST THING(S) YOU ATE:

SERVICE

. . . .

① ② ③ ④ ⑤

THE ONE THING YOU'LL NEVER FORGET:

EAT HERE AGAIN?   YES ☐   NO ☐   IF DESPERATE ☐

HOLE IN THE WALLS

AKA: DIVES & DINERS

NAME OF THE RESTAURANT

NUMBER

065

PSST: ADD THIS TO THE INDEX(ES) IN THE BACK SO YOU CAN FIND IT QUICKLY LATER

WHERE WAS IT LOCATED?

CITY: STATE/COUNTRY:

WHY DID YOU EAT HERE?

☐ HEARD GREAT THINGS   FORCED AGAINST WILL ☐

☐ IT LOOKED GOOD   HUNGRY & DESPERATE ☐

☐ ONLY THING OPEN   WAS DRUNK ☐

OTHER:

THE BEST THING(S) YOU ATE:

. . . .

THE WORST THING(S) YOU ATE:

. . . .

~ AMBIANCE
① ② ③ ④ ⑤

FOOD
① ② ③ ④ ⑤

SERVICE
① ② ③ ④ ⑤

THE ONE THING YOU'LL NEVER FORGET:

EAT HERE AGAIN?   YES ☐   NO ☐   IF DESPERATE ☐

NUMBER

066

NAME OF THE RESTAURANT

PSST: ADD THIS TO THE INDEX(ES) IN THE BACK SO YOU CAN FIND IT QUICKLY LATER

WHERE WAS IT LOCATED?

CITY: STATE/COUNTRY:

WHY DID YOU EAT HERE?

- [ ] HEARD GREAT THINGS
- [ ] IT LOOKED GOOD
- [ ] ONLY THING OPEN

- [ ] FORCED AGAINST WILL
- [ ] HUNGRY & DESPERATE
- [ ] WAS DRUNK

OTHER:

AMBIANCE
① ② ③ ④ ⑤

FOOD
① ② ③ ④ ⑤

SERVICE
① ② ③ ④ ⑤

THE BEST THING(S) YOU ATE:
. . . .

THE WORST THING(S) YOU ATE:
. . . .

THE ONE THING YOU'LL NEVER FORGET:

EAT HERE AGAIN?   YES [ ]   NO [ ]   IF DESPERATE [ ]

HOLE IN THE WALLS

AKA: DIVES & DINERS

NAME OF THE RESTAURANT

NUMBER

067

PSST: ADD THIS TO THE INDEX(ES) IN THE BACK SO YOU CAN FIND IT QUICKLY LATER

WHERE WAS IT LOCATED?

CITY:

STATE/COUNTRY:

WHY DID YOU EAT HERE?

☐ HEARD GREAT THINGS

FORCED AGAINST WILL ☐

☐ IT LOOKED GOOD

HUNGRY & DESPERATE ☐

☐ ONLY THING OPEN

WAS DRUNK ☐

OTHER:

THE BEST THING(S) YOU ATE:

. . . .

THE WORST THING(S) YOU ATE:

. . . .

AMBIANCE
① ② ③ ④ ⑤

FOOD
① ② ③ ④ ⑤

SERVICE
① ② ③ ④ ⑤

THE ONE THING YOU'LL NEVER FORGET:

EAT HERE AGAIN?   YES ☐   NO ☐   IF DESPERATE ☐

☐ BEEN THERE

THE STATION INN

402 12TH AVENUE SOUTH, NASHVILLE, TN 37203

A FEW FAVORITES

☐ A THING OF POPCORN

☐ HOT DOGS

☐ PIMENTO CHEESE

NON-BEER DRINKS
① ② ③ ④ ⑤

BLUEGRASS MUSIC
① ② ③ ④ ⑤

THIS TINY MUSIC VENUE OPENED IN 1974, AND WE'D
WAGER TO BET THAT NOT A THING HAS CHANGED SINCE.
IT'S PROBABLY NOT FOR EVERYONE—BUT THAT'S WHAT
MAKES IT SO AMAZING. THE PLACE ISN'T MUCH BIGGER
THAN A LIVING ROOM. THE WALLS ARE COVERED WITH
WOOD PANELING. THE CROWD SITS IN FOLDING CHAIRS,
LISTENS TO MUSIC, AND ORDERS 'THINGS OF POPCORN'
AND HOT DOGS FROM A COUNTER THAT MIGHT AS WELL
HAVE BEEN YOUR GRANDPA'S KITCHEN. IT'S MAGICAL.

☐ BEEN THERE

KITTY'S CAFE

810 1/2 EAST 31ST STREET, KANSAS CITY, MO 64109

A FEW FAVORITES

☐ PORK TENDERLOIN SANDWICHES

☐ TATER TOTS

☐ DOUBLE CHEESEBURGERS

CLAUSTROPHOBIA
① ② ③ ④ ⑤

PESKY 'AMBIANCE'
① ② ③ ④ ⑤

THIS PLACE IS CASH ONLY AND YOU CAN'T EAT (OR
BARELY STAND) INSIDE—NOT THAT YOU WOULD WANT TO
ANYWAY, SINCE IT'S THE SIZE OF A ROOMY JAIL CELL.
BUT DON'T LET THAT STOP YOU FROM ENJOYING THE
BEST PORK TENDERLOIN SANDWICHES KNOWN TO MAN.
THEY'RE THINLY SLICED, PILED HIGH, & FRIED TO A
LIGHT CRISP—JUST GET THERE EARLY OR THE LINE WILL
BE AROUND THE BLOCK. PSST: DON'T TRY TO BE SMART
& ORDER AHEAD—THEY DON'T HAVE A PHONE.

HOLE IN THE WALLS

AKA: DIVES & DINERS

NAME OF THE RESTAURANT

NUMBER

068

PSST: ADD THIS TO THE INDEX(ES) IN THE BACK SO YOU CAN FIND IT QUICKLY LATER

WHERE WAS IT LOCATED?

CITY: STATE/COUNTRY:

WHY DID YOU EAT HERE?

- [ ] HEARD GREAT THINGS
- [ ] IT LOOKED GOOD
- [ ] ONLY THING OPEN
- [ ] FORCED AGAINST WILL
- [ ] HUNGRY & DESPERATE
- [ ] WAS DRUNK

OTHER:

THE BEST THING(S) YOU ATE:

. . . .

THE WORST THING(S) YOU ATE:

. . . .

AMBIANCE
(1) (2) (3) (4) (5)

FOOD
(1) (2) (3) (4) (5)

SERVICE
(1) (2) (3) (4) (5)

THE ONE THING YOU'LL NEVER FORGET:

EAT HERE AGAIN? YES [ ] NO [ ] IF DESPERATE [ ]

HOLE IN THE WALLS

NUMBER

069

NAME OF THE RESTAURANT

PSST: ADD THIS TO THE INDEX(ES) IN THE BACK SO YOU CAN FIND IT QUICKLY LATER

WHERE WAS IT LOCATED?

CITY: STATE/COUNTRY:

WHY DID YOU EAT HERE?

☐ HEARD GREAT THINGS   FORCED AGAINST WILL ☐

☐ IT LOOKED GOOD   HUNGRY & DESPERATE ☐

☐ ONLY THING OPEN   WAS DRUNK ☐

OTHER:

AMBIANCE

① ② ③ ④ ⑤

THE BEST THING(S) YOU ATE:

. . . .

FOOD

① ② ③ ④ ⑤

THE WORST THING(S) YOU ATE:

. . . .

SERVICE

① ② ③ ④ ⑤

THE ONE THING YOU'LL NEVER FORGET:

EAT HERE AGAIN?   YES ☐   NO ☐   IF DESPERATE ☐

HOLE IN THE WALLS
AKA: DIVES & DINERS

NAME OF THE RESTAURANT

NUMBER

070

PSST: ADD THIS TO THE INDEX(ES) IN THE BACK SO YOU CAN FIND IT QUICKLY LATER

WHERE WAS IT LOCATED?

CITY: STATE/COUNTRY:

WHY DID YOU EAT HERE?

☐ HEARD GREAT THINGS   FORCED AGAINST WILL ☐

☐ IT LOOKED GOOD   HUNGRY & DESPERATE ☐

☐ ONLY THING OPEN   WAS DRUNK ☐

OTHER:

THE BEST THING(S) YOU ATE:

. . . .

AMBIANCE
① ② ③ ④ ⑤

FOOD
① ② ③ ④ ⑤

THE WORST THING(S) YOU ATE:

. . . .

SERVICE
① ② ③ ④ ⑤

THE ONE THING YOU'LL NEVER FORGET:

EAT HERE AGAIN?   YES ☐   NO ☐   IF DESPERATE ☐

NUMBER

071

NAME OF THE RESTAURANT

PSST: ADD THIS TO THE INDEX(ES) IN THE BACK SO YOU CAN FIND IT QUICKLY LATER

WHERE WAS IT LOCATED?

CITY: STATE/COUNTRY:

WHY DID YOU EAT HERE?

☐ HEARD GREAT THINGS   FORCED AGAINST WILL ☐

☐ IT LOOKED GOOD   HUNGRY & DESPERATE ☐

☐ ONLY THING OPEN   WAS DRUNK ☐

OTHER:

AMBIANCE

① ② ③ ④ ⑤

FOOD

① ② ③ ④ ⑤

SERVICE

① ② ③ ④ ⑤

THE BEST THING(S) YOU ATE:

. . . .

THE WORST THING(S) YOU ATE:

. . . .

THE ONE THING YOU'LL NEVER FORGET:

EAT HERE AGAIN?   YES ☐   NO ☐   IF DESPERATE ☐

HOLE IN THE WALLS
AKA: DIVES & DINERS

NAME OF THE RESTAURANT

NUMBER

072

PSST: ADD THIS TO THE INDEX(ES) IN THE BACK SO YOU CAN FIND IT QUICKLY LATER

WHERE WAS IT LOCATED?

CITY: STATE/COUNTRY:

WHY DID YOU EAT HERE?

- [ ] HEARD GREAT THINGS
- [ ] IT LOOKED GOOD
- [ ] ONLY THING OPEN
- [ ] FORCED AGAINST WILL
- [ ] HUNGRY & DESPERATE
- [ ] WAS DRUNK

OTHER:

THE BEST THING(S) YOU ATE:

. . . .

THE WORST THING(S) YOU ATE:

. . . .

AMBIANCE
(1) (2) (3) (4) (5)

FOOD
(1) (2) (3) (4) (5)

SERVICE
(1) (2) (3) (4) (5)

THE ONE THING YOU'LL NEVER FORGET:

EAT HERE AGAIN?　　YES [ ]　NO [ ]　IF DESPERATE [ ]

NUMBER

073

NAME OF THE RESTAURANT

PSST: ADD THIS TO THE INDEX(ES) IN THE BACK SO YOU CAN FIND IT QUICKLY LATER

WHERE WAS IT LOCATED?

CITY: STATE/COUNTRY:

WHY DID YOU EAT HERE?

☐ HEARD GREAT THINGS FORCED AGAINST WILL ☐

☐ IT LOOKED GOOD HUNGRY & DESPERATE ☐

☐ ONLY THING OPEN WAS DRUNK ☐

OTHER:

AMBIANCE

① ② ③ ④ ⑤

FOOD

① ② ③ ④ ⑤

SERVICE

① ② ③ ④ ⑤

THE BEST THING(S) YOU ATE:

. . . .

THE WORST THING(S) YOU ATE:

. . . .

THE ONE THING YOU'LL NEVER FORGET:

EAT HERE AGAIN? YES ☐ NO ☐ IF DESPERATE ☐

HOLE IN THE WALLS
AKA: DIVES & DINERS

NAME OF THE RESTAURANT

NUMBER

074

PSST: ADD THIS TO THE INDEX(ES) IN THE BACK SO YOU CAN FIND IT QUICKLY LATER

WHERE WAS IT LOCATED?

CITY: STATE/COUNTRY:

WHY DID YOU EAT HERE?

☐ HEARD GREAT THINGS   FORCED AGAINST WILL ☐

☐ IT LOOKED GOOD   HUNGRY & DESPERATE ☐

☐ ONLY THING OPEN   WAS DRUNK ☐

OTHER:

THE BEST THING(S) YOU ATE:

. . . .

AMBIANCE
① ② ③ ④ ⑤

FOOD
① ② ③ ④ ⑤

THE WORST THING(S) YOU ATE:

. . . .

SERVICE
① ② ③ ④ ⑤

THE ONE THING YOU'LL NEVER FORGET:

EAT HERE AGAIN?   YES ☐   NO ☐   IF DESPERATE ☐

THE CHEESEBURGER

NATIONAL CHEESEBURGER DAY IS ON SEPTEMBER 18TH

PERFECT FOR	TERRIBLE FOR
☐ LAST MEALS (PRE-DIET)	EATING SALADS NEAR ☐
☐ LAST MEALS (PRE-DEATH)	PORTION CONTROL ☐

A BONUS BURGER: SINCE THIS IS THE 'DINERS & DIVES'
SECTION, WE COULDN'T TECHNICALLY INCLUDE THIS
ONE—IT'S NOT EVEN CLOSE TO A DIVE. THAT SAID, NO
LIST OF AMAZING CHEESEBURGERS WOULD BE COMPLETE
WITHOUT THE EMILY BURGER AT 'EMILY' IN NEW YORK,
NY. IT'S PRICEY—BUT SOOOO WORTH IT. TRUST US.

FIND NOTABLES AT: | **LOCATION**

☐ TUCKER'S ONION BURGERS	OKLAHOMA CITY, OK
☐ LE TUB SALOON	HOLLYWOOD, CA
☐ CALLAGHAN'S IRISH SOCIAL CLUB	MOBILE, AL
☐ THE BURGER DIVE	BILLINGS, MT
☐ BUB'S NOLA	NEW ORLEANS, LA
☐ EL HONESTO MIKE	PROVIDENCIA, CHILE
☐ JACK BROWN'S	HARRISONBURG, VA
☐ EASEY'S	COLLINGWOOD, AUSTRALIA
☐ THE NOOK	ST. PAUL, MN
☐ J.G. MELON	NEW YORK, NY
☐ THE APPLE PAN	LOS ANGELES, CA
☐ MR. BARTLEY'S BURGER COTTAGE	CAMBRIDGE, MA

WRITE-IN CANDIDATES

HOLE IN THE WALLS
AKA: DIVES & DINERS

NAME OF THE RESTAURANT

NUMBER

075

PSST: ADD THIS TO THE INDEX(ES) IN THE BACK SO YOU CAN FIND IT QUICKLY LATER

WHERE WAS IT LOCATED?

CITY: STATE/COUNTRY:

WHY DID YOU EAT HERE?

- [ ] HEARD GREAT THINGS
- [ ] IT LOOKED GOOD
- [ ] ONLY THING OPEN

- FORCED AGAINST WILL [ ]
- HUNGRY & DESPERATE [ ]
- WAS DRUNK [ ]

OTHER:

THE BEST THING(S) YOU ATE:

. . . .

AMBIANCE
① ② ③ ④ ⑤

FOOD
① ② ③ ④ ⑤

THE WORST THING(S) YOU ATE:

. . . .

SERVICE
① ② ③ ④ ⑤

THE ONE THING YOU'LL NEVER FORGET:

EAT HERE AGAIN?   YES [ ]   NO [ ]   IF DESPERATE [ ]

NUMBER

076

NAME OF THE RESTAURANT

PSST: ADD THIS TO THE INDEX(ES) IN THE BACK SO YOU CAN FIND IT QUICKLY LATER

WHERE WAS IT LOCATED?

CITY: STATE/COUNTRY:

WHY DID YOU EAT HERE?

- [ ] HEARD GREAT THINGS
- [ ] IT LOOKED GOOD
- [ ] ONLY THING OPEN
- [ ] FORCED AGAINST WILL
- [ ] HUNGRY & DESPERATE
- [ ] WAS DRUNK

OTHER:

AMBIANCE
① ② ③ ④ ⑤

FOOD
① ② ③ ④ ⑤

SERVICE
① ② ③ ④ ⑤

THE BEST THING(S) YOU ATE:
. . . .

THE WORST THING(S) YOU ATE:
. . . .

THE ONE THING YOU'LL NEVER FORGET:

EAT HERE AGAIN?   YES [ ]   NO [ ]   IF DESPERATE [ ]

HOLE IN THE WALLS
AKA: DIVES & DINERS

NAME OF THE RESTAURANT

NUMBER

077

PSST: ADD THIS TO THE INDEX(ES) IN THE BACK SO YOU CAN FIND IT QUICKLY LATER

WHERE WAS IT LOCATED?

CITY: STATE/COUNTRY:

WHY DID YOU EAT HERE?

- [ ] HEARD GREAT THINGS
- [ ] IT LOOKED GOOD
- [ ] ONLY THING OPEN
- [ ] FORCED AGAINST WILL
- [ ] HUNGRY & DESPERATE
- [ ] WAS DRUNK

OTHER:

THE BEST THING(S) YOU ATE:

. . . .

THE WORST THING(S) YOU ATE:

. . . .

AMBIANCE
(1) (2) (3) (4) (5)

FOOD
(1) (2) (3) (4) (5)

SERVICE
(1) (2) (3) (4) (5)

THE ONE THING YOU'LL NEVER FORGET:

EAT HERE AGAIN?   YES [ ]   NO [ ]   IF DESPERATE [ ]

NUMBER

078

NAME OF THE RESTAURANT

PSST: ADD THIS TO THE INDEX(ES) IN THE BACK SO YOU CAN FIND IT QUICKLY LATER

WHERE WAS IT LOCATED?

CITY: STATE/COUNTRY:

WHY DID YOU EAT HERE?

☐ HEARD GREAT THINGS   FORCED AGAINST WILL ☐

☐ IT LOOKED GOOD   HUNGRY & DESPERATE ☐

☐ ONLY THING OPEN   WAS DRUNK ☐

OTHER:

AMBIANCE

① ② ③ ④ ⑤

FOOD

① ② ③ ④ ⑤

SERVICE

① ② ③ ④ ⑤

THE BEST THING(S) YOU ATE:

. . . .

THE WORST THING(S) YOU ATE:

. . . .

THE ONE THING YOU'LL NEVER FORGET:

EAT HERE AGAIN?   YES ☐   NO ☐   IF DESPERATE ☐

HOLE IN THE WALLS
AKA: DIVES & DINERS

NAME OF THE RESTAURANT

NUMBER

079

PSST: ADD THIS TO THE INDEX(ES) IN THE BACK SO YOU CAN FIND IT QUICKLY LATER

WHERE WAS IT LOCATED?

CITY: STATE/COUNTRY:

WHY DID YOU EAT HERE?

- [ ] HEARD GREAT THINGS
- [ ] IT LOOKED GOOD
- [ ] ONLY THING OPEN
- [ ] FORCED AGAINST WILL
- [ ] HUNGRY & DESPERATE
- [ ] WAS DRUNK

OTHER:

THE BEST THING(S) YOU ATE:

. . . .

THE WORST THING(S) YOU ATE:

. . . .

AMBIANCE
① ② ③ ④ ⑤

FOOD
① ② ③ ④ ⑤

SERVICE
① ② ③ ④ ⑤

THE ONE THING YOU'LL NEVER FORGET:

EAT HERE AGAIN?   YES [ ]   NO [ ]   IF DESPERATE [ ]

NUMBER

080

NAME OF THE RESTAURANT

PSST: ADD THIS TO THE INDEX(ES) IN THE BACK SO YOU CAN FIND IT QUICKLY LATER

WHERE WAS IT LOCATED?

CITY: STATE/COUNTRY:

WHY DID YOU EAT HERE?

- [ ] HEARD GREAT THINGS
- [ ] IT LOOKED GOOD
- [ ] ONLY THING OPEN
- [ ] FORCED AGAINST WILL
- [ ] HUNGRY & DESPERATE
- [ ] WAS DRUNK

OTHER:

AMBIANCE
① ② ③ ④ ⑤

FOOD
① ② ③ ④ ⑤

SERVICE
① ② ③ ④ ⑤

THE BEST THING(S) YOU ATE:

. . . .

THE WORST THING(S) YOU ATE:

. . . .

THE ONE THING YOU'LL NEVER FORGET:

EAT HERE AGAIN?   YES [ ]   NO [ ]   IF DESPERATE [ ]

HOLE IN THE WALLS
AKA: DIVES & DINERS

NAME OF THE RESTAURANT

NUMBER

081

PSST: ADD THIS TO THE INDEX(ES) IN THE BACK SO YOU CAN FIND IT QUICKLY LATER

WHERE WAS IT LOCATED?

CITY: STATE/COUNTRY:

WHY DID YOU EAT HERE?

- [ ] HEARD GREAT THINGS
- [ ] IT LOOKED GOOD
- [ ] ONLY THING OPEN

- FORCED AGAINST WILL [ ]
- HUNGRY & DESPERATE [ ]
- WAS DRUNK [ ]

OTHER:

THE BEST THING(S) YOU ATE:

. . . .

AMBIANCE
(1) (2) (3) (4) (5)

FOOD
(1) (2) (3) (4) (5)

THE WORST THING(S) YOU ATE:

. . . .

SERVICE
(1) (2) (3) (4) (5)

THE ONE THING YOU'LL NEVER FORGET:

EAT HERE AGAIN?   YES [ ]   NO [ ]   IF DESPERATE [ ]

A FEW MUST-TRYS

RESTAURANT	LOCATION
☐ JOE'S COFFEE SHOP	SAN FRANCISCO, CA
☐ FRANKS DINER	KENOSHA, WI
☐ NIECIE'S RESTAURANT	KANSAS CITY, MO
☐ TRAVIS COFFEE SHOP	ST. CLAIR SHORES, MI
☐ PANINI PETE'S	FAIRHOPE, AL
☐ SUPER DUPER WEENIE	FAIRFIELD, CT
☐ STEER-IN	INDIANAPOLIS, IN
☐ THE BLUE BENN	BENNINGTON, VT
☐ TICK TOCK DINER	CLIFTON, NJ
☐ THE SILVER SKILLET	ATLANTA, GA
☐ MEMPHIS BARBECUE COMPANY	HORN LAKE, MS
☐ DELUCA'S DINER	PITTSBURGH, PA
☐ TUNE-UP CAFÉ	SANTA FE, NM
☐ 11TH STREET DINER	MIAMI BEACH, FL
☐ TEL-WINK GRILL	HOUSTON, TX
☐ BLACKBIRD WOODFIRE	FARGO, ND
☐ LEONARD'S PIT BARBECUE	MEMPHIS, TN
☐ COZY DOG	SPRINGFIELD, IL
☐ VICTOR'S 1959 CAFE	MINNEAPOLIS, MN
☐ GOOD DOG BAR	PHILADELPHIA, PA
☐ GALLEY DINER	SOUTH BOSTON, MA
☐ UNCLE MIKE'S PLACE	CHICAGO, IL
☐ FAT CHOY RESTAURANT	LAS VEGAS, NV
☐ HILLBILLY HOT DOGS	LESAGE, WV

WRITE-IN CANDIDATES

HOLE IN THE WALLS

AKA: DIVES & DINERS

NAME OF THE RESTAURANT

NUMBER

082

PSST: ADD THIS TO THE INDEX(ES) IN THE BACK SO YOU CAN FIND IT QUICKLY LATER

WHERE WAS IT LOCATED?

CITY: STATE/COUNTRY:

WHY DID YOU EAT HERE?

☐ HEARD GREAT THINGS   FORCED AGAINST WILL ☐
☐ IT LOOKED GOOD   HUNGRY & DESPERATE ☐
☐ ONLY THING OPEN   WAS DRUNK ☐

OTHER:

THE BEST THING(S) YOU ATE:

. . . .

THE WORST THING(S) YOU ATE:

. . . .

AMBIANCE
① ② ③ ④ ⑤

FOOD
① ② ③ ④ ⑤

SERVICE
① ② ③ ④ ⑤

THE ONE THING YOU'LL NEVER FORGET:

EAT HERE AGAIN?   YES ☐   NO ☐   IF DESPERATE ☐

NUMBER

083

NAME OF THE RESTAURANT

PSST: ADD THIS TO THE INDEX(ES) IN THE BACK SO YOU CAN FIND IT QUICKLY LATER

WHERE WAS IT LOCATED?

CITY: STATE/COUNTRY:

WHY DID YOU EAT HERE?

- [ ] HEARD GREAT THINGS
- [ ] IT LOOKED GOOD
- [ ] ONLY THING OPEN
- [ ] FORCED AGAINST WILL
- [ ] HUNGRY & DESPERATE
- [ ] WAS DRUNK

OTHER:

AMBIANCE
(1) (2) (3) (4) (5)

FOOD
(1) (2) (3) (4) (5)

SERVICE
(1) (2) (3) (4) (5)

THE BEST THING(S) YOU ATE:

. . . .

THE WORST THING(S) YOU ATE:

. . . .

THE ONE THING YOU'LL NEVER FORGET:

EAT HERE AGAIN? YES [ ] NO [ ] IF DESPERATE [ ]

HOLE IN THE WALLS
AKA: DIVES & DINERS

NAME OF THE RESTAURANT

NUMBER

084

PSST: ADD THIS TO THE INDEX(ES) IN THE BACK SO YOU CAN FIND IT QUICKLY LATER

WHERE WAS IT LOCATED?

CITY: STATE/COUNTRY:

WHY DID YOU EAT HERE?

☐ HEARD GREAT THINGS   FORCED AGAINST WILL ☐
☐ IT LOOKED GOOD   HUNGRY & DESPERATE ☐
☐ ONLY THING OPEN   WAS DRUNK ☐

OTHER:

THE BEST THING(S) YOU ATE:

. . . .

AMBIANCE
① ② ③ ④ ⑤

FOOD
① ② ③ ④ ⑤

THE WORST THING(S) YOU ATE:

. . . .

SERVICE
① ② ③ ④ ⑤

THE ONE THING YOU'LL NEVER FORGET:

EAT HERE AGAIN?   YES ☐   NO ☐   IF DESPERATE ☐

NUMBER

085

NAME OF THE RESTAURANT

PSST: ADD THIS TO THE INDEX(ES) IN THE BACK SO YOU CAN FIND IT QUICKLY LATER

WHERE WAS IT LOCATED?

CITY:　　　　　STATE/COUNTRY:

WHY DID YOU EAT HERE?

☐ HEARD GREAT THINGS　　　FORCED AGAINST WILL ☐

☐ IT LOOKED GOOD　　　HUNGRY & DESPERATE ☐

☐ ONLY THING OPEN　　　　　　　WAS DRUNK ☐

OTHER:

AMBIANCE

① ② ③ ④ ⑤

FOOD

① ② ③ ④ ⑤

SERVICE

① ② ③ ④ ⑤

THE BEST THING(S) YOU ATE:

. . . .

THE WORST THING(S) YOU ATE:

. . . .

THE ONE THING YOU'LL NEVER FORGET:

EAT HERE AGAIN?　　YES ☐　　NO ☐　　IF DESPERATE ☐

HOLE IN THE WALLS
AKA: DIVES & DINERS

NAME OF THE RESTAURANT

NUMBER

086

PSST: ADD THIS TO THE INDEX(ES) IN THE BACK SO YOU CAN FIND IT QUICKLY LATER

WHERE WAS IT LOCATED?

CITY: STATE/COUNTRY:

WHY DID YOU EAT HERE?

☐ HEARD GREAT THINGS FORCED AGAINST WILL ☐
☐ IT LOOKED GOOD HUNGRY & DESPERATE ☐
☐ ONLY THING OPEN WAS DRUNK ☐

OTHER:

THE BEST THING(S) YOU ATE:

. . . .

AMBIANCE
① ② ③ ④ ⑤

FOOD
① ② ③ ④ ⑤

THE WORST THING(S) YOU ATE:

. . . .

SERVICE
① ② ③ ④ ⑤

THE ONE THING YOU'LL NEVER FORGET:

EAT HERE AGAIN? YES ☐ NO ☐ IF DESPERATE ☐

NUMBER

087

NAME OF THE RESTAURANT

PSST: ADD THIS TO THE INDEX(ES) IN THE BACK SO YOU CAN FIND IT QUICKLY LATER

WHERE WAS IT LOCATED?

CITY: STATE/COUNTRY:

WHY DID YOU EAT HERE?

- [ ] HEARD GREAT THINGS
- [ ] IT LOOKED GOOD
- [ ] ONLY THING OPEN

- FORCED AGAINST WILL [ ]
- HUNGRY & DESPERATE [ ]
- WAS DRUNK [ ]

OTHER:

AMBIANCE
(1) (2) (3) (4) (5)

FOOD
(1) (2) (3) (4) (5)

SERVICE
(1) (2) (3) (4) (5)

THE BEST THING(S) YOU ATE:

. . . .

THE WORST THING(S) YOU ATE:

. . . .

THE ONE THING YOU'LL NEVER FORGET:

EAT HERE AGAIN?   YES [ ]   NO [ ]   IF DESPERATE [ ]

HOLE IN THE WALLS

AKA: DIVES & DINERS

NAME OF THE RESTAURANT

NUMBER

088

PSST: ADD THIS TO THE INDEX(ES) IN THE BACK SO YOU CAN FIND IT QUICKLY LATER

WHERE WAS IT LOCATED?

CITY: STATE/COUNTRY:

WHY DID YOU EAT HERE?

- [ ] HEARD GREAT THINGS
- [ ] IT LOOKED GOOD
- [ ] ONLY THING OPEN
- [ ] FORCED AGAINST WILL
- [ ] HUNGRY & DESPERATE
- [ ] WAS DRUNK

OTHER:

THE BEST THING(S) YOU ATE:

. . . .

THE WORST THING(S) YOU ATE:

. . . .

AMBIANCE
(1) (2) (3) (4) (5)

FOOD
(1) (2) (3) (4) (5)

SERVICE
(1) (2) (3) (4) (5)

THE ONE THING YOU'LL NEVER FORGET:

EAT HERE AGAIN?   YES [ ]   NO [ ]   IF DESPERATE [ ]

TAKE A FOOD TOUR

CHICAGO, IL

HOME TO MORE THAN 7,300 RESTAURANTS

NOT-TO-MISS CHICAGO 'SPECIALTIES'

- [ ] DEEP-DISH PIZZA
- [ ] CHICAGO-STYLE POPCORN
- [ ] CHICKEN VESUVIO
- [ ] CHICAGO DOGS

THE OLDEST RESTAURANT IN CHICAGO JUST SO HAPPENS TO BE A DINER. 'DALEY'S' FIRST OPENED IN 1892, AND HAS BEEN IN OPERATION EVER SINCE—ALTHOUGH IT DID MOVE ACROSS THE STREET IN 2019.

RESTAURANT	KNOWN FOR
[ ] WHITE PALACE GRILL	PATTY MELTS
[ ] HOPLEAF	THE CB & J
[ ] ELEVEN CITY DINER	PASTRAMI SANDWICHES
[ ] DANCEN	BULDAK
[ ] DOVE'S LUNCHEONETTE	BURNT ENDS HASH
[ ] RICE'N BREAD	GREASY ASIAN FOOD
[ ] KIMSKI	POLISH SAUSAGE
[ ] PUB ROYALE	SAMOSAS
[ ] DINER GRILL	THE SLINGER
[ ] JAKE MELNICK'S CORNER TAP	CHICKEN WINGS
[ ] CLUB LUCKY	ITALIAN FOOD
[ ] AU CHEVAL	FRIED BOLOGNA
[ ] ROCK ISLAND PUBLIC HOUSE	KOREAN BBQ BALLS

WRITE-IN CANDIDATES

HOLE IN THE WALLS AKA: DIVES & DINERS

NAME OF THE RESTAURANT

NUMBER

O89

PSST: ADD THIS TO THE INDEX(ES) IN THE BACK SO YOU CAN FIND IT QUICKLY LATER

WHERE WAS IT LOCATED?

CITY: STATE/COUNTRY:

WHY DID YOU EAT HERE?

☐ HEARD GREAT THINGS   FORCED AGAINST WILL ☐
☐ IT LOOKED GOOD   HUNGRY & DESPERATE ☐
☐ ONLY THING OPEN   WAS DRUNK ☐

OTHER:

THE BEST THING(S) YOU ATE:

. . . .

AMBIANCE
① ② ③ ④ ⑤

FOOD
① ② ③ ④ ⑤

THE WORST THING(S) YOU ATE:

. . . .

SERVICE
① ② ③ ④ ⑤

THE ONE THING YOU'LL NEVER FORGET:

EAT HERE AGAIN?   YES ☐   NO ☐   IF DESPERATE ☐

NUMBER

090

NAME OF THE RESTAURANT

PSST: ADD THIS TO THE INDEX(ES) IN THE BACK SO YOU CAN FIND IT QUICKLY LATER

WHERE WAS IT LOCATED?

CITY: STATE/COUNTRY:

WHY DID YOU EAT HERE?

☐ HEARD GREAT THINGS   FORCED AGAINST WILL ☐

☐ IT LOOKED GOOD   HUNGRY & DESPERATE ☐

☐ ONLY THING OPEN   WAS DRUNK ☐

OTHER:

AMBIANCE

① ② ③ ④ ⑤

FOOD

① ② ③ ④ ⑤

SERVICE

① ② ③ ④ ⑤

THE BEST THING(S) YOU ATE:

. . . .

THE WORST THING(S) YOU ATE:

. . . .

THE ONE THING YOU'LL NEVER FORGET:

EAT HERE AGAIN?   YES ☐   NO ☐   IF DESPERATE ☐

PAINFULLY COOL

PAINFULLY COOL

AKA: HIPSTER SPOTS

NAME OF THE RESTAURANT

NUMBER

091

PSST: ADD THIS TO THE INDEX(ES) IN THE BACK SO YOU CAN FIND IT QUICKLY LATER

WHERE WAS IT LOCATED?

CITY: STATE/COUNTRY:

WHY DID YOU EAT HERE?

- [ ] HEARD GREAT THINGS
- [ ] IT LOOKED GOOD
- [ ] ONLY THING OPEN
- [ ] FORCED AGAINST WILL
- [ ] HUNGRY & DESPERATE
- [ ] WAS DRUNK

OTHER:

THE BEST THING(S) YOU ATE:

. . . .

AMBIANCE
(1) (2) (3) (4) (5)

FOOD
(1) (2) (3) (4) (5)

THE WORST THING(S) YOU ATE:

. . . .

SERVICE
(1) (2) (3) (4) (5)

THE ONE THING YOU'LL NEVER FORGET:

EAT HERE AGAIN?   YES [ ]   NO [ ]   IF DESPERATE [ ]

NUMBER

092

NAME OF THE RESTAURANT

PSST: ADD THIS TO THE INDEX(ES) IN THE BACK SO YOU CAN FIND IT QUICKLY LATER

WHERE WAS IT LOCATED?

CITY: STATE/COUNTRY:

WHY DID YOU EAT HERE?

- [ ] HEARD GREAT THINGS
- [ ] IT LOOKED GOOD
- [ ] ONLY THING OPEN
- [ ] FORCED AGAINST WILL
- [ ] HUNGRY & DESPERATE
- [ ] WAS DRUNK

OTHER:

AMBIANCE
① ② ③ ④ ⑤

FOOD
① ② ③ ④ ⑤

SERVICE
① ② ③ ④ ⑤

THE BEST THING(S) YOU ATE:
. . . .

THE WORST THING(S) YOU ATE:
. . . .

THE ONE THING YOU'LL NEVER FORGET:

EAT HERE AGAIN?   YES [ ]   NO [ ]   IF DESPERATE [ ]

PAINFULLY COOL

NAME OF THE RESTAURANT

NUMBER

093

PSST: ADD THIS TO THE INDEX(ES) IN THE BACK SO YOU CAN FIND IT QUICKLY LATER

WHERE WAS IT LOCATED?

CITY: STATE/COUNTRY:

WHY DID YOU EAT HERE?

- [ ] HEARD GREAT THINGS
- [ ] IT LOOKED GOOD
- [ ] ONLY THING OPEN
- [ ] FORCED AGAINST WILL
- [ ] HUNGRY & DESPERATE
- [ ] WAS DRUNK

OTHER:

THE BEST THING(S) YOU ATE:

. . . .

AMBIANCE
① ② ③ ④ ⑤

FOOD
① ② ③ ④ ⑤

THE WORST THING(S) YOU ATE:

. . . .

SERVICE
① ② ③ ④ ⑤

THE ONE THING YOU'LL NEVER FORGET:

EAT HERE AGAIN?   YES [ ]   NO [ ]   IF DESPERATE [ ]

NUMBER

094

NAME OF THE RESTAURANT

PSST: ADD THIS TO THE INDEX(ES) IN THE BACK SO YOU CAN FIND IT QUICKLY LATER

WHERE WAS IT LOCATED?

CITY: STATE/COUNTRY:

WHY DID YOU EAT HERE?

☐ HEARD GREAT THINGS   FORCED AGAINST WILL ☐

☐ IT LOOKED GOOD   HUNGRY & DESPERATE ☐

☐ ONLY THING OPEN   WAS DRUNK ☐

OTHER:

AMBIANCE

① ② ③ ④ ⑤

FOOD

① ② ③ ④ ⑤

SERVICE

① ② ③ ④ ⑤

THE BEST THING(S) YOU ATE:

. . . .

THE WORST THING(S) YOU ATE:

. . . .

THE ONE THING YOU'LL NEVER FORGET:

EAT HERE AGAIN?   YES ☐   NO ☐   IF DESPERATE ☐

NAME OF THE RESTAURANT

NUMBER

095

PSST: ADD THIS TO THE INDEX(ES) IN THE BACK SO YOU CAN FIND IT QUICKLY LATER

WHERE WAS IT LOCATED?

CITY: STATE/COUNTRY:

WHY DID YOU EAT HERE?

- [ ] HEARD GREAT THINGS
- [ ] IT LOOKED GOOD
- [ ] ONLY THING OPEN
- [ ] FORCED AGAINST WILL
- [ ] HUNGRY & DESPERATE
- [ ] WAS DRUNK

OTHER:

THE BEST THING(S) YOU ATE:

. . . .

THE WORST THING(S) YOU ATE:

. . . .

AMBIANCE
(1) (2) (3) (4) (5)

FOOD
(1) (2) (3) (4) (5)

SERVICE
(1) (2) (3) (4) (5)

THE ONE THING YOU'LL NEVER FORGET:

EAT HERE AGAIN? YES [ ] NO [ ] IF DESPERATE [ ]

PAINFULLY COOL

NUMBER

096

NAME OF THE RESTAURANT

PSST: ADD THIS TO THE INDEX(ES) IN THE BACK SO YOU CAN FIND IT QUICKLY LATER

WHERE WAS IT LOCATED?

CITY: STATE/COUNTRY:

WHY DID YOU EAT HERE?

☐ HEARD GREAT THINGS   FORCED AGAINST WILL ☐

☐ IT LOOKED GOOD   HUNGRY & DESPERATE ☐

☐ ONLY THING OPEN   WAS DRUNK ☐

OTHER:

AMBIANCE
① ② ③ ④ ⑤

FOOD
① ② ③ ④ ⑤

SERVICE
① ② ③ ④ ⑤

THE BEST THING(S) YOU ATE:
. . . .

THE WORST THING(S) YOU ATE:
. . . .

THE ONE THING YOU'LL NEVER FORGET:

EAT HERE AGAIN?   YES ☐   NO ☐   IF DESPERATE ☐

NAME OF THE RESTAURANT

NUMBER

097

PSST: ADD THIS TO THE INDEX(ES) IN THE BACK SO YOU CAN FIND IT QUICKLY LATER

WHERE WAS IT LOCATED?

CITY: STATE/COUNTRY:

WHY DID YOU EAT HERE?

☐ HEARD GREAT THINGS   FORCED AGAINST WILL ☐

☐ IT LOOKED GOOD   HUNGRY & DESPERATE ☐

☐ ONLY THING OPEN   WAS DRUNK ☐

OTHER:

THE BEST THING(S) YOU ATE:

. . . .

AMBIANCE

① ② ③ ④ ⑤

FOOD

① ② ③ ④ ⑤

THE WORST THING(S) YOU ATE:

. . . .

SERVICE

① ② ③ ④ ⑤

THE ONE THING YOU'LL NEVER FORGET:

EAT HERE AGAIN?   YES ☐   NO ☐   IF DESPERATE ☐

☐ BEEN THERE

1803 NYC

82 READE STREET, NEW YORK, NY 10007

A FEW FAVORITES

☐ THE GUMBO
☐ THE GUMBO
☐ AND THE GUMBO

COOL WALLPAPER
① ② ③ ④ ⑤

TINY BALCONIES
① ② ③ ④ ⑤

WHENEVER WE'RE IN NEW YORK AND FEEL LIKE GOING SOMEWHERE EFFORTLESSLY INTERESTING—THIS IS WHERE WE GO. IT'S A BEAUTIFUL PLACE, BUT NOT FUSSY OR OVERLY DESIGNED. IT'S JUST FUN TO BE HERE. THERE'S A TINY (AND WE MEAN TINY) BALCONY INSIDE WHERE MUSICIANS WILL PLAY OCCASIONALLY. THERE'S VINTAGE WALLPAPER COVERING A FEW WALLS. I'D SAY THAT WE COME HERE FOR THE FOOD—BUT REALLY IT'S JUST A BONUS TO AN ALREADY GREAT EXPERIENCE.

☐ BEEN THERE

NEPTUNE OYSTER

63 SALEM STREET #1, BOSTON, MA 02113

A FEW FAVORITES

☐ ISLAND CREEK OYSTERS
☐ HOT BUTTER LOBSTER ROLL
☐ CLAM CHOWDER

RESERVATIONS
⓪ ① ② ③ ④

LINES AT 11AM
① ② ③ ④ ⑤

THIS TINY PLACE IS A MUST VISIT FOR US WHENEVER WE'RE EVEN CLOSE TO BOSTON. THAT IS REALLY SAYING A LOT CONSIDERING: A) WE HATE STANDING IN LINES, B) WE HATE CROWDS, AND C) ONE OF US IS ALLERGIC TO SEAFOOD. I'M NOT EVEN EXAGGERATING WHEN I SAY THAT A MEMBER OF OUR TEAM ACTIVELY DREAMS ABOUT THE HOT BUTTER LOBSTER ROLL HERE. HEY, I PROBABLY WOULD TOO IF IT WEREN'T FOR THE WHOLE, YOU KNOW, ALLERGIC THING. ANYWAY, JUST GET THERE EARLY.

PAINFULLY COOL

AKA: HIPSTER SPOTS

NAME OF THE RESTAURANT

NUMBER

098

PSST: ADD THIS TO THE INDEX(ES) IN THE BACK SO YOU CAN FIND IT QUICKLY LATER

WHERE WAS IT LOCATED?

CITY: STATE/COUNTRY:

WHY DID YOU EAT HERE?

- [ ] HEARD GREAT THINGS
- [ ] IT LOOKED GOOD
- [ ] ONLY THING OPEN
- [ ] FORCED AGAINST WILL
- [ ] HUNGRY & DESPERATE
- [ ] WAS DRUNK

OTHER:

THE BEST THING(S) YOU ATE:

. . . .

THE WORST THING(S) YOU ATE:

. . . .

AMBIANCE
(1) (2) (3) (4) (5)

FOOD
(1) (2) (3) (4) (5)

SERVICE
(1) (2) (3) (4) (5)

THE ONE THING YOU'LL NEVER FORGET:

EAT HERE AGAIN?   YES [ ]   NO [ ]   IF DESPERATE [ ]

PAINFULLY COOL

NUMBER

099

NAME OF THE RESTAURANT

PSST: ADD THIS TO THE INDEX(ES) IN THE BACK SO YOU CAN FIND IT QUICKLY LATER

WHERE WAS IT LOCATED?

CITY: STATE/COUNTRY:

WHY DID YOU EAT HERE?

- [ ] HEARD GREAT THINGS
- [ ] IT LOOKED GOOD
- [ ] ONLY THING OPEN
- [ ] FORCED AGAINST WILL
- [ ] HUNGRY & DESPERATE
- [ ] WAS DRUNK

OTHER:

AMBIANCE
(1) (2) (3) (4) (5)

FOOD
(1) (2) (3) (4) (5)

SERVICE
(1) (2) (3) (4) (5)

THE BEST THING(S) YOU ATE:
. . . .

THE WORST THING(S) YOU ATE:
. . . .

THE ONE THING YOU'LL NEVER FORGET:

EAT HERE AGAIN? YES [ ] NO [ ] IF DESPERATE [ ]

NAME OF THE RESTAURANT

NUMBER

100

PSST: ADD THIS TO THE INDEX(ES) IN THE BACK SO YOU CAN FIND IT QUICKLY LATER

WHERE WAS IT LOCATED?

CITY: STATE/COUNTRY:

WHY DID YOU EAT HERE?

☐ HEARD GREAT THINGS   FORCED AGAINST WILL ☐

☐ IT LOOKED GOOD   HUNGRY & DESPERATE ☐

☐ ONLY THING OPEN   WAS DRUNK ☐

OTHER:

THE BEST THING(S) YOU ATE:

. . . .

AMBIANCE
① ② ③ ④ ⑤

FOOD
① ② ③ ④ ⑤

THE WORST THING(S) YOU ATE:

. . . .

SERVICE
① ② ③ ④ ⑤

THE ONE THING YOU'LL NEVER FORGET:

EAT HERE AGAIN?   YES ☐   NO ☐   IF DESPERATE ☐

NUMBER

101

NAME OF THE RESTAURANT

PSST: ADD THIS TO THE INDEX(ES) IN THE BACK SO YOU CAN FIND IT QUICKLY LATER

WHERE WAS IT LOCATED?

CITY: STATE/COUNTRY:

WHY DID YOU EAT HERE?

- [ ] HEARD GREAT THINGS
- [ ] IT LOOKED GOOD
- [ ] ONLY THING OPEN
- [ ] FORCED AGAINST WILL
- [ ] HUNGRY & DESPERATE
- [ ] WAS DRUNK

OTHER:

AMBIANCE
(1) (2) (3) (4) (5)

FOOD
(1) (2) (3) (4) (5)

SERVICE
(1) (2) (3) (4) (5)

THE BEST THING(S) YOU ATE:

. . . .

THE WORST THING(S) YOU ATE:

. . . .

THE ONE THING YOU'LL NEVER FORGET:

EAT HERE AGAIN? YES [ ] NO [ ] IF DESPERATE [ ]

PAINFULLY COOL

AKA: HIPSTER SPOTS

NAME OF THE RESTAURANT

NUMBER

102

PSST: ADD THIS TO THE INDEX(ES) IN THE BACK SO YOU CAN FIND IT QUICKLY LATER

WHERE WAS IT LOCATED?

CITY: STATE/COUNTRY:

WHY DID YOU EAT HERE?

- [ ] HEARD GREAT THINGS
- [ ] IT LOOKED GOOD
- [ ] ONLY THING OPEN
- [ ] FORCED AGAINST WILL
- [ ] HUNGRY & DESPERATE
- [ ] WAS DRUNK

OTHER:

THE BEST THING(S) YOU ATE:

. . . .

THE WORST THING(S) YOU ATE:

. . . .

AMBIANCE
(1) (2) (3) (4) (5)

FOOD
(1) (2) (3) (4) (5)

SERVICE
(1) (2) (3) (4) (5)

THE ONE THING YOU'LL NEVER FORGET:

EAT HERE AGAIN? YES [ ] NO [ ] IF DESPERATE [ ]

NUMBER

103

NAME OF THE RESTAURANT

PSST: ADD THIS TO THE INDEX(ES) IN THE BACK SO YOU CAN FIND IT QUICKLY LATER

WHERE WAS IT LOCATED?

CITY: STATE/COUNTRY:

WHY DID YOU EAT HERE?

- [ ] HEARD GREAT THINGS
- [ ] IT LOOKED GOOD
- [ ] ONLY THING OPEN

- [ ] FORCED AGAINST WILL
- [ ] HUNGRY & DESPERATE
- [ ] WAS DRUNK

OTHER:

AMBIANCE
① ② ③ ④ ⑤

FOOD
① ② ③ ④ ⑤

SERVICE
① ② ③ ④ ⑤

THE BEST THING(S) YOU ATE:
. . . .

THE WORST THING(S) YOU ATE:
. . . .

THE ONE THING YOU'LL NEVER FORGET:

EAT HERE AGAIN?   YES [ ]   NO [ ]   IF DESPERATE [ ]

NAME OF THE RESTAURANT

NUMBER

104

PSST: ADD THIS TO THE INDEX(ES) IN THE BACK SO YOU CAN FIND IT QUICKLY LATER

WHERE WAS IT LOCATED?

CITY: STATE/COUNTRY:

WHY DID YOU EAT HERE?

- [ ] HEARD GREAT THINGS
- [ ] IT LOOKED GOOD
- [ ] ONLY THING OPEN
- [ ] FORCED AGAINST WILL
- [ ] HUNGRY & DESPERATE
- [ ] WAS DRUNK

OTHER:

THE BEST THING(S) YOU ATE:

. . . .

THE WORST THING(S) YOU ATE:

. . . .

AMBIANCE
(1) (2) (3) (4) (5)

FOOD
(1) (2) (3) (4) (5)

SERVICE
(1) (2) (3) (4) (5)

THE ONE THING YOU'LL NEVER FORGET:

EAT HERE AGAIN?   YES [ ]   NO [ ]   IF DESPERATE [ ]

PHOTOGENIC INTERIORS

PLACES TO TAKE PHOTOS—AND MAYBE EAT OR WHATEVER

PERFECT FOR	TERRIBLE FOR
☐ IMPRESSING FRIENDS	NOT BEING A TOURIST ☐
☐ ANNOYING FRIENDS	EMBARRASSMENT ☐

IS THE FOOD ANY GOOD? MAYBE. WHO KNOWS. LET'S BE HONEST, EVERYONE IS HERE FOR THE SAME REASON—TO TAKE HIGHLY CRAFTED PHOTOS THAT LOOK EFFORTLESS SO THEY CAN ALL HUMBLE-BRAG TO THEIR FRIENDS AND FAMILY. THESE PLACES CAN'T BE BEAT FOR ADDING A DASH OF VISUAL-JEALOUSLY TO YOUR VACATION.

FIND SOME GREAT VIEWS AT:	LOCATION
☐ PIETRO NOLITA	NEW YORK, NY
☐ MAMEY MIAMI	CORAL GABLES, FL
☐ WILMOTT'S GHOST	SEATTLE, WA
☐ THE SALTRY	HALIBUT COVE, AK
☐ MEROIS	WEST HOLLYWOOD, CA
☐ SWIFT & SONS	CHICAGO, IL
☐ EL PINTO RESTAURANT	ALBUQUERQUE, NM
☐ ZOU ZOU'S	NEW YORK, NY
☐ RECESS	ATLANTA, GA
☐ KOSUSHI MIAMI	MIAMI BEACH, FL
☐ OCHO	DALLAS, TX
☐ BUDDAKAN	NEW YORK, NY

WRITE-IN CANDIDATES

NAME OF THE RESTAURANT

NUMBER

105

PSST: ADD THIS TO THE INDEX(ES) IN THE BACK SO YOU CAN FIND IT QUICKLY LATER

WHERE WAS IT LOCATED?

CITY: STATE/COUNTRY:

WHY DID YOU EAT HERE?

- [ ] HEARD GREAT THINGS
- [ ] IT LOOKED GOOD
- [ ] ONLY THING OPEN

- FORCED AGAINST WILL [ ]
- HUNGRY & DESPERATE [ ]
- WAS DRUNK [ ]

OTHER:

THE BEST THING(S) YOU ATE:

. . . .

AMBIANCE
① ② ③ ④ ⑤

FOOD
① ② ③ ④ ⑤

THE WORST THING(S) YOU ATE:

. . . .

SERVICE
① ② ③ ④ ⑤

THE ONE THING YOU'LL NEVER FORGET:

EAT HERE AGAIN? YES [ ] NO [ ] IF DESPERATE [ ]

NUMBER

106

NAME OF THE RESTAURANT

PSST: ADD THIS TO THE INDEX(ES) IN THE BACK SO YOU CAN FIND IT QUICKLY LATER

WHERE WAS IT LOCATED?

CITY: STATE/COUNTRY:

WHY DID YOU EAT HERE?

- [ ] HEARD GREAT THINGS
- [ ] IT LOOKED GOOD
- [ ] ONLY THING OPEN

FORCED AGAINST WILL [ ]
HUNGRY & DESPERATE [ ]
WAS DRUNK [ ]

OTHER:

AMBIANCE
(1) (2) (3) (4) (5)

THE BEST THING(S) YOU ATE:

. . . .

FOOD
(1) (2) (3) (4) (5)

THE WORST THING(S) YOU ATE:

SERVICE
(1) (2) (3) (4) (5)

. . . .

THE ONE THING YOU'LL NEVER FORGET:

EAT HERE AGAIN?   YES [ ]   NO [ ]   IF DESPERATE [ ]

PAINFULLY COOL

NAME OF THE RESTAURANT

NUMBER

107

PSST: ADD THIS TO THE INDEX(ES) IN THE BACK SO YOU CAN FIND IT QUICKLY LATER

WHERE WAS IT LOCATED?

CITY: STATE/COUNTRY:

WHY DID YOU EAT HERE?

☐ HEARD GREAT THINGS   FORCED AGAINST WILL ☐

☐ IT LOOKED GOOD   HUNGRY & DESPERATE ☐

☐ ONLY THING OPEN   WAS DRUNK ☐

OTHER:

THE BEST THING(S) YOU ATE:

. . . .

THE WORST THING(S) YOU ATE:

. . . .

AMBIANCE
① ② ③ ④ ⑤

FOOD
① ② ③ ④ ⑤

SERVICE
① ② ③ ④ ⑤

THE ONE THING YOU'LL NEVER FORGET:

EAT HERE AGAIN?   YES ☐   NO ☐   IF DESPERATE ☐

NUMBER
108

NAME OF THE RESTAURANT

PSST: ADD THIS TO THE INDEX(ES) IN THE BACK SO YOU CAN FIND IT QUICKLY LATER

WHERE WAS IT LOCATED?

CITY: STATE/COUNTRY:

WHY DID YOU EAT HERE?

☐ HEARD GREAT THINGS   FORCED AGAINST WILL ☐
☐ IT LOOKED GOOD   HUNGRY & DESPERATE ☐
☐ ONLY THING OPEN   WAS DRUNK ☐

OTHER:

AMBIANCE
① ② ③ ④ ⑤

FOOD
① ② ③ ④ ⑤

SERVICE
① ② ③ ④ ⑤

THE BEST THING(S) YOU ATE:
. . . .

THE WORST THING(S) YOU ATE:
. . . .

THE ONE THING YOU'LL NEVER FORGET:

EAT HERE AGAIN?   YES ☐   NO ☐   IF DESPERATE ☐

PAINFULLY COOL

AKA: HIPSTER SPOTS

NAME OF THE RESTAURANT

NUMBER

109

PSST: ADD THIS TO THE INDEX(ES) IN THE BACK SO YOU CAN FIND IT QUICKLY LATER

WHERE WAS IT LOCATED?

CITY: STATE/COUNTRY:

WHY DID YOU EAT HERE?

- [ ] HEARD GREAT THINGS
- [ ] IT LOOKED GOOD
- [ ] ONLY THING OPEN

- FORCED AGAINST WILL [ ]
- HUNGRY & DESPERATE [ ]
- WAS DRUNK [ ]

OTHER:

THE BEST THING(S) YOU ATE:

. . . .

THE WORST THING(S) YOU ATE:

. . . .

AMBIANCE
(1) (2) (3) (4) (5)

FOOD
(1) (2) (3) (4) (5)

SERVICE
(1) (2) (3) (4) (5)

THE ONE THING YOU'LL NEVER FORGET:

EAT HERE AGAIN?   YES [ ]   NO [ ]   IF DESPERATE [ ]

NUMBER

NAME OF THE RESTAURANT

110

PSST: ADD THIS TO THE INDEX(ES) IN THE BACK SO YOU CAN FIND IT QUICKLY LATER

WHERE WAS IT LOCATED?

CITY: STATE/COUNTRY:

WHY DID YOU EAT HERE?

- [ ] HEARD GREAT THINGS
- [ ] IT LOOKED GOOD
- [ ] ONLY THING OPEN
- [ ] FORCED AGAINST WILL
- [ ] HUNGRY & DESPERATE
- [ ] WAS DRUNK

OTHER:

AMBIANCE
① ② ③ ④ ⑤

FOOD
① ② ③ ④ ⑤

SERVICE
① ② ③ ④ ⑤

THE BEST THING(S) YOU ATE:

. . . .

THE WORST THING(S) YOU ATE:

. . . .

THE ONE THING YOU'LL NEVER FORGET:

EAT HERE AGAIN? YES [ ] NO [ ] IF DESPERATE [ ]

PAINFULLY COOL

NAME OF THE RESTAURANT

NUMBER

111

PSST: ADD THIS TO THE INDEX(ES) IN THE BACK SO YOU CAN FIND IT QUICKLY LATER

WHERE WAS IT LOCATED?

CITY: STATE/COUNTRY:

WHY DID YOU EAT HERE?

- [ ] HEARD GREAT THINGS
- [ ] IT LOOKED GOOD
- [ ] ONLY THING OPEN

- FORCED AGAINST WILL [ ]
- HUNGRY & DESPERATE [ ]
- WAS DRUNK [ ]

OTHER:

THE BEST THING(S) YOU ATE:

. . . .

THE WORST THING(S) YOU ATE:

. . . .

AMBIANCE
(1) (2) (3) (4) (5)

FOOD
(1) (2) (3) (4) (5)

SERVICE
(1) (2) (3) (4) (5)

THE ONE THING YOU'LL NEVER FORGET:

EAT HERE AGAIN?   YES [ ]   NO [ ]   IF DESPERATE [ ]

A FEW MUST-TRYS

RESTAURANT	LOCATION
☐ THE KITCHEN	JACKSON HOLE, WY
☐ CAFE MUTTON	HUDSON, NY
☐ SENATE	BLUE ASH, OH
☐ LENGUA MADRE	NEW ORLEANS, LA
☐ PARADIS BOOKS & BREAD	NORTH MIAMI, FL
☐ SUPPERLAND	CHARLOTTE, NC
☐ MA DER LAO KITCHEN	OKLAHOMA CITY, OK
☐ JŪN BY KIN	HOUSTON, TX
☐ BIRDIE'S	AUSTIN, TX
☐ DEAR ANNIE	CAMBRIDGE, MA
☐ MID-CITY RESTAURANT	CINCINNATI, OH
☐ KINGFISHER	SAN DIEGO, CA
☐ AUDREY	NASHVILLE, TN
☐ GOOD GOOD CULTURE CLUB	SAN FRANCISCO, CA
☐ MISTER MAO	NEW ORLEANS, LA
☐ IRWIN'S	PHILADELPHIA, PA
☐ REGARDS	PORTLAND, ME
☐ BACANORA	PHOENIX, AZ
☐ QUARTER SHEETS PIZZA	LOS ANGELES, CA
☐ EVETTE'S	CHICAGO, IL
☐ LOS FÉLIX	MIAMI, FL
☐ YANGBAN SOCIETY	LOS ANGELES, CA
☐ THE CAMPGROUND	KANSAS CITY, MO
☐ DAYTRIP	OAKLAND, CA

WRITE-IN CANDIDATES

PAINFULLY COOL

NAME OF THE RESTAURANT

NUMBER

112

PSST: ADD THIS TO THE INDEX(ES) IN THE BACK SO YOU CAN FIND IT QUICKLY LATER

WHERE WAS IT LOCATED?

CITY: STATE/COUNTRY:

WHY DID YOU EAT HERE?

☐ HEARD GREAT THINGS   FORCED AGAINST WILL ☐
☐ IT LOOKED GOOD   HUNGRY & DESPERATE ☐
☐ ONLY THING OPEN   WAS DRUNK ☐

OTHER:

THE BEST THING(S) YOU ATE:

AMBIANCE
① ② ③ ④ ⑤

FOOD
① ② ③ ④ ⑤

THE WORST THING(S) YOU ATE:

SERVICE
① ② ③ ④ ⑤

THE ONE THING YOU'LL NEVER FORGET:

EAT HERE AGAIN?   YES ☐   NO ☐   IF DESPERATE ☐

PAINFULLY COOL

NUMBER

113

NAME OF THE RESTAURANT

PSST: ADD THIS TO THE INDEX(ES) IN THE BACK SO YOU CAN FIND IT QUICKLY LATER

WHERE WAS IT LOCATED?

CITY: STATE/COUNTRY:

WHY DID YOU EAT HERE?

☐ HEARD GREAT THINGS   FORCED AGAINST WILL ☐

☐ IT LOOKED GOOD   HUNGRY & DESPERATE ☐

☐ ONLY THING OPEN   WAS DRUNK ☐

OTHER:

AMBIANCE
① ② ③ ④ ⑤

FOOD
① ② ③ ④ ⑤

SERVICE
① ② ③ ④ ⑤

THE BEST THING(S) YOU ATE:

. . . .

THE WORST THING(S) YOU ATE:

. . . .

THE ONE THING YOU'LL NEVER FORGET:

EAT HERE AGAIN?   YES ☐   NO ☐   IF DESPERATE ☐

NAME OF THE RESTAURANT

NUMBER

114

PSST: ADD THIS TO THE INDEX(ES) IN THE BACK SO YOU CAN FIND IT QUICKLY LATER

WHERE WAS IT LOCATED?

CITY: STATE/COUNTRY:

WHY DID YOU EAT HERE?

☐ HEARD GREAT THINGS   FORCED AGAINST WILL ☐
☐ IT LOOKED GOOD   HUNGRY & DESPERATE ☐
☐ ONLY THING OPEN   WAS DRUNK ☐

OTHER:

THE BEST THING(S) YOU ATE:

. . . .

AMBIANCE
① ② ③ ④ ⑤

FOOD
① ② ③ ④ ⑤

THE WORST THING(S) YOU ATE:

. . . .

SERVICE
① ② ③ ④ ⑤

THE ONE THING YOU'LL NEVER FORGET:

EAT HERE AGAIN?   YES ☐   NO ☐   IF DESPERATE ☐

NUMBER

115

NAME OF THE RESTAURANT

PSST: ADD THIS TO THE INDEX(ES) IN THE BACK SO YOU CAN FIND IT QUICKLY LATER

WHERE WAS IT LOCATED?

CITY: STATE/COUNTRY:

WHY DID YOU EAT HERE?

- [ ] HEARD GREAT THINGS
- [ ] IT LOOKED GOOD
- [ ] ONLY THING OPEN
- [ ] FORCED AGAINST WILL
- [ ] HUNGRY & DESPERATE
- [ ] WAS DRUNK

OTHER:

AMBIANCE
① ② ③ ④ ⑤

FOOD
① ② ③ ④ ⑤

SERVICE
① ② ③ ④ ⑤

THE BEST THING(S) YOU ATE:
. . . .

THE WORST THING(S) YOU ATE:
. . . .

THE ONE THING YOU'LL NEVER FORGET:

EAT HERE AGAIN?   YES [ ]   NO [ ]   IF DESPERATE [ ]

NAME OF THE RESTAURANT

NUMBER

116

PSST: ADD THIS TO THE INDEX(ES) IN THE BACK SO YOU CAN FIND IT QUICKLY LATER

WHERE WAS IT LOCATED?

CITY: STATE/COUNTRY:

WHY DID YOU EAT HERE?

- [ ] HEARD GREAT THINGS
- [ ] IT LOOKED GOOD
- [ ] ONLY THING OPEN

FORCED AGAINST WILL [ ]
HUNGRY & DESPERATE [ ]
WAS DRUNK [ ]

OTHER:

THE BEST THING(S) YOU ATE:

. . . .

AMBIANCE
(1) (2) (3) (4) (5)

FOOD
(1) (2) (3) (4) (5)

THE WORST THING(S) YOU ATE:

. . . .

SERVICE
(1) (2) (3) (4) (5)

THE ONE THING YOU'LL NEVER FORGET:

EAT HERE AGAIN?   YES [ ]   NO [ ]   IF DESPERATE [ ]

PAINFULLY COOL

NUMBER

117

NAME OF THE RESTAURANT

PSST: ADD THIS TO THE INDEX(ES) IN THE BACK SO YOU CAN FIND IT QUICKLY LATER

WHERE WAS IT LOCATED?

CITY: STATE/COUNTRY:

WHY DID YOU EAT HERE?

☐ HEARD GREAT THINGS   FORCED AGAINST WILL ☐
☐ IT LOOKED GOOD   HUNGRY & DESPERATE ☐
☐ ONLY THING OPEN   WAS DRUNK ☐

OTHER:

AMBIANCE
① ② ③ ④ ⑤

FOOD
① ② ③ ④ ⑤

SERVICE
① ② ③ ④ ⑤

THE BEST THING(S) YOU ATE:
. . . .

THE WORST THING(S) YOU ATE:
. . . .

THE ONE THING YOU'LL NEVER FORGET:

EAT HERE AGAIN?   YES ☐   NO ☐   IF DESPERATE ☐

NAME OF THE RESTAURANT

NUMBER

118

PSST: ADD THIS TO THE INDEX(ES) IN THE BACK SO YOU CAN FIND IT QUICKLY LATER

WHERE WAS IT LOCATED?

CITY: STATE/COUNTRY:

WHY DID YOU EAT HERE?

☐ HEARD GREAT THINGS   FORCED AGAINST WILL ☐

☐ IT LOOKED GOOD   HUNGRY & DESPERATE ☐

☐ ONLY THING OPEN   WAS DRUNK ☐

OTHER:

THE BEST THING(S) YOU ATE:

. . . .

THE WORST THING(S) YOU ATE:

. . . .

AMBIANCE

① ② ③ ④ ⑤

FOOD

① ② ③ ④ ⑤

SERVICE

① ② ③ ④ ⑤

THE ONE THING YOU'LL NEVER FORGET:

EAT HERE AGAIN?   YES ☐   NO ☐   IF DESPERATE ☐

NEW YORK, NY

RANKED THE SECOND BEST FOOD CITY IN AMERICA (2023)

A HIPSTER RESTAURANT CHECKLIST

- [ ] OLD FASHIONED LIGHTS
- [ ] EXPOSED DUCTWORK
- A LACK OF PLATES [ ]
- NO UNIFORMS [ ]

WHAT MAKES FOR THE PERFECT 'HIPSTER SPOT'? WELL, FOR US, IT'S A PLACE WITH AMBIANCE THAT IS JUST AS AMAZING AS THE FOOD (WHICH *COUGH* SHOULD BE AMAZING). THESE PLACES WON'T DISAPPOINT.

RESTAURANT	KNOWN FOR
[ ] DEPT OF CULTURE	NIGERIAN TASTING MENU
[ ] MOTEL MORRIS	MALT VINEGAR FRIES
[ ] C AS IN CHARLIE	POPCORN CHICKEN
[ ] JACK'S WIFE FREDA	ROSEWATER WAFFLES
[ ] BONNIE'S	CANTONESE AMERICAN
[ ] THE MARSHAL	MEATLOAF
[ ] WHITE TIGER	KOREAN FRIED CHICKEN
[ ] POMMES FRITES	POUTINE
[ ] DHAMAKA	GURDA KAPOORA
[ ] BOBWHITE COUNTER	CHICKEN SANDWICHES
[ ] WHILE WE WERE YOUNG	DRINKS IN LITTLE BIRDS
[ ] FREEMANS	DEVILS ON HORSEBACK
[ ] TONCHIN	TONKOTSU RAMEN

WRITE-IN CANDIDATES

NAME OF THE RESTAURANT

NUMBER

119

PSST: ADD THIS TO THE INDEX(ES) IN THE BACK SO YOU CAN FIND IT QUICKLY LATER

WHERE WAS IT LOCATED?

CITY: STATE/COUNTRY:

WHY DID YOU EAT HERE?

- [ ] HEARD GREAT THINGS
- [ ] IT LOOKED GOOD
- [ ] ONLY THING OPEN
- [ ] FORCED AGAINST WILL
- [ ] HUNGRY & DESPERATE
- [ ] WAS DRUNK

OTHER:

THE BEST THING(S) YOU ATE:

THE WORST THING(S) YOU ATE:

AMBIANCE
(1) (2) (3) (4) (5)

FOOD
(1) (2) (3) (4) (5)

SERVICE
(1) (2) (3) (4) (5)

THE ONE THING YOU'LL NEVER FORGET:

EAT HERE AGAIN?   YES [ ]   NO [ ]   IF DESPERATE [ ]

NUMBER

120

NAME OF THE RESTAURANT

PSST: ADD THIS TO THE INDEX(ES) IN THE BACK SO YOU CAN FIND IT QUICKLY LATER

WHERE WAS IT LOCATED?

CITY: STATE/COUNTRY:

WHY DID YOU EAT HERE?

- [ ] HEARD GREAT THINGS
- [ ] IT LOOKED GOOD
- [ ] ONLY THING OPEN
- [ ] FORCED AGAINST WILL
- [ ] HUNGRY & DESPERATE
- [ ] WAS DRUNK

OTHER:

AMBIANCE
(1) (2) (3) (4) (5)

FOOD
(1) (2) (3) (4) (5)

SERVICE
(1) (2) (3) (4) (5)

THE BEST THING(S) YOU ATE:
. . . .

THE WORST THING(S) YOU ATE:
. . . .

THE ONE THING YOU'LL NEVER FORGET:

EAT HERE AGAIN? YES [ ] NO [ ] IF DESPERATE [ ]

MOTHER APPROVED

MOTHER APPROVED

AKA: CHAINS

NAME OF THE RESTAURANT

NUMBER

121

PSST: ADD THIS TO THE INDEX(ES) IN THE BACK SO YOU CAN FIND IT QUICKLY LATER

WHERE WAS IT LOCATED?

CITY: _____ STATE/COUNTRY: _____

WHY DID YOU EAT HERE?

- [ ] HEARD GREAT THINGS
- [ ] IT LOOKED GOOD
- [ ] ONLY THING OPEN

- [ ] FORCED AGAINST WILL
- [ ] HUNGRY & DESPERATE
- [ ] WAS DRUNK

OTHER:

THE BEST THING(S) YOU ATE:

....

AMBIANCE
(1) (2) (3) (4) (5)

FOOD
(1) (2) (3) (4) (5)

THE WORST THING(S) YOU ATE:

....

SERVICE
(1) (2) (3) (4) (5)

THE ONE THING YOU'LL NEVER FORGET:

EAT HERE AGAIN?   YES [ ]   NO [ ]   IF DESPERATE [ ]

MOTHER APPROVED

NUMBER

122

NAME OF THE RESTAURANT

PSST: ADD THIS TO THE INDEX(ES) IN THE BACK SO YOU CAN FIND IT QUICKLY LATER

WHERE WAS IT LOCATED?

CITY: STATE/COUNTRY:

WHY DID YOU EAT HERE?

- [ ] HEARD GREAT THINGS
- [ ] IT LOOKED GOOD
- [ ] ONLY THING OPEN
- [ ] FORCED AGAINST WILL
- [ ] HUNGRY & DESPERATE
- [ ] WAS DRUNK

OTHER:

AMBIANCE
(1) (2) (3) (4) (5)

FOOD
(1) (2) (3) (4) (5)

SERVICE
(1) (2) (3) (4) (5)

THE BEST THING(S) YOU ATE:

. . . .

THE WORST THING(S) YOU ATE:

. . . .

THE ONE THING YOU'LL NEVER FORGET:

EAT HERE AGAIN? YES [ ] NO [ ] IF DESPERATE [ ]

MOTHER APPROVED

AKA: CHAINS

NAME OF THE RESTAURANT

NUMBER

123

PSST: ADD THIS TO THE INDEX(ES) IN THE BACK SO YOU CAN FIND IT QUICKLY LATER

WHERE WAS IT LOCATED?

CITY: STATE/COUNTRY:

WHY DID YOU EAT HERE?

- [ ] HEARD GREAT THINGS
- [ ] IT LOOKED GOOD
- [ ] ONLY THING OPEN

FORCED AGAINST WILL [ ]
HUNGRY & DESPERATE [ ]
WAS DRUNK [ ]

OTHER:

THE BEST THING(S) YOU ATE:

. . . .

THE WORST THING(S) YOU ATE:

. . . .

AMBIANCE
(1) (2) (3) (4) (5)

FOOD
(1) (2) (3) (4) (5)

SERVICE
(1) (2) (3) (4) (5)

THE ONE THING YOU'LL NEVER FORGET:

EAT HERE AGAIN?   YES [ ]   NO [ ]   IF DESPERATE [ ]

MOTHER APPROVED

NUMBER
124

NAME OF THE RESTAURANT

PSST: ADD THIS TO THE INDEX(ES) IN THE BACK SO YOU CAN FIND IT QUICKLY LATER

WHERE WAS IT LOCATED?

CITY: STATE/COUNTRY:

WHY DID YOU EAT HERE?

- [ ] HEARD GREAT THINGS
- [ ] IT LOOKED GOOD
- [ ] ONLY THING OPEN
- [ ] FORCED AGAINST WILL
- [ ] HUNGRY & DESPERATE
- [ ] WAS DRUNK

OTHER:

AMBIANCE
(1) (2) (3) (4) (5)

FOOD
(1) (2) (3) (4) (5)

SERVICE
(1) (2) (3) (4) (5)

THE BEST THING(S) YOU ATE:
. . . .

THE WORST THING(S) YOU ATE:
. . . .

THE ONE THING YOU'LL NEVER FORGET:

EAT HERE AGAIN?   YES [ ]   NO [ ]   IF DESPERATE [ ]

MOTHER APPROVED

AKA: CHAINS

NAME OF THE RESTAURANT

NUMBER

125

PSST: ADD THIS TO THE INDEX(ES) IN THE BACK SO YOU CAN FIND IT QUICKLY LATER

WHERE WAS IT LOCATED?

CITY: STATE/COUNTRY:

WHY DID YOU EAT HERE?

- [ ] HEARD GREAT THINGS
- [ ] IT LOOKED GOOD
- [ ] ONLY THING OPEN
- [ ] FORCED AGAINST WILL
- [ ] HUNGRY & DESPERATE
- [ ] WAS DRUNK

OTHER:

THE BEST THING(S) YOU ATE:

. . . .

AMBIANCE
(1) (2) (3) (4) (5)

FOOD
(1) (2) (3) (4) (5)

THE WORST THING(S) YOU ATE:

. . . .

SERVICE
(1) (2) (3) (4) (5)

THE ONE THING YOU'LL NEVER FORGET:

EAT HERE AGAIN?   YES [ ]   NO [ ]   IF DESPERATE [ ]

MOTHER APPROVED

NUMBER

126

NAME OF THE RESTAURANT

PSST: ADD THIS TO THE INDEX(ES) IN THE BACK SO YOU CAN FIND IT QUICKLY LATER

WHERE WAS IT LOCATED?

CITY: STATE/COUNTRY:

WHY DID YOU EAT HERE?

- ☐ HEARD GREAT THINGS
- ☐ IT LOOKED GOOD
- ☐ ONLY THING OPEN

- FORCED AGAINST WILL ☐
- HUNGRY & DESPERATE ☐
- WAS DRUNK ☐

OTHER:

AMBIANCE

① ② ③ ④ ⑤

FOOD

① ② ③ ④ ⑤

SERVICE

① ② ③ ④ ⑤

THE BEST THING(S) YOU ATE:

. . . .

THE WORST THING(S) YOU ATE:

. . . .

THE ONE THING YOU'LL NEVER FORGET:

EAT HERE AGAIN?   YES ☐   NO ☐   IF DESPERATE ☐

MOTHER APPROVED

NAME OF THE RESTAURANT

NUMBER

127

PSST: ADD THIS TO THE INDEX(ES) IN THE BACK SO YOU CAN FIND IT QUICKLY LATER

WHERE WAS IT LOCATED?

CITY: STATE/COUNTRY:

WHY DID YOU EAT HERE?

- [ ] HEARD GREAT THINGS
- [ ] IT LOOKED GOOD
- [ ] ONLY THING OPEN
- [ ] FORCED AGAINST WILL
- [ ] HUNGRY & DESPERATE
- [ ] WAS DRUNK

OTHER:

THE BEST THING(S) YOU ATE:

. . . .

THE WORST THING(S) YOU ATE:

. . . .

AMBIANCE
(1) (2) (3) (4) (5)

FOOD
(1) (2) (3) (4) (5)

SERVICE
(1) (2) (3) (4) (5)

THE ONE THING YOU'LL NEVER FORGET:

EAT HERE AGAIN?   YES [ ]   NO [ ]   IF DESPERATE [ ]

OUR FAVORITES

☐ **BEEN THERE**   ## SKYLINE CHILI

LOCATIONS IN FL, IN, KY, AND OH

A FEW FAVORITES   INNUENDOS
① ② ③ ④ ⑤

☐ THREE-WAYS

☐ FOUR-WAYS   SHREDDED CHEESE

☐ FIVE-WAYS   ① ② ③ ④ ⑪

PEOPLE EITHER LOVE OR HATE THIS SMALL REGIONAL
CHAIN, BUT WE DON'T KNOW WHAT'S NOT TO LIKE
ABOUT PLATES OF SPAGHETTI NOODLES COVERED WITH
MOUNTAINS OF EVER-SO-SLIGHTLY SWEET CHILI AND
SHREDDED CHEESE—AKA, A THREE-WAY. YOU CAN ALSO
GET IT AS A FOUR OR FIVE-WAY (WHICH ADDS BEANS
AND/OR ONIONS) BUT WE PREFER THE CLASSIC. DON'T
SLEEP ON THE CONEY DOGS EITHER—WE'D HAVE LISTED
IT ABOVE, BUT WE COULDN'T RESIST THE SEX JOKES.

☐ **BEEN THERE**   ## HAWAIIAN BROS

LOCATIONS IN AR, AZ, IL, IA, KS, MO, NY, AND OK

A FEW FAVORITES   SPAM APPETIZERS
① ② ③ ④ ⑤

☐ LUAU PIG PLATE LUNCH

☐ HULI HULI PLATE LUNCH   REALIZING IT'S 'BROS'

☐ DOLE WHIPS   ① ② ③ ④ ⑤

CONFESSION TIME: WE'VE EATEN AT THIS PLACE FOR
YEARS—EVER SINCE THE FIRST LOCATION POPPED UP IN
2018, A LITTLE OUTSIDE OF TOWN. THEIR FOOD IS SO
SIMPLE, YET SO DELICIOUS. SO IT WAS A LITTLE HARD
TO TAKE WHEN, JUST A FEW WEEKS AGO, WE HEARD A
RADIO AD & FOUND OUT THAT THEIR NAME IS ACTUALLY
'HAWAIIAN BROS' AND NOT 'HAWAIIAN BROTHERS.' WE
THOUGHT IT WAS JUST ABBREVIATED IN THE LOGO. ICK.
WE STILL LOVE IT THOUGH—EVEN IF THEY ARE BROS.

MOTHER APPROVED

AKA: CHAINS

NAME OF THE RESTAURANT

NUMBER

128

PSST: ADD THIS TO THE INDEX(ES) IN THE BACK SO YOU CAN FIND IT QUICKLY LATER

WHERE WAS IT LOCATED?

CITY: STATE/COUNTRY:

WHY DID YOU EAT HERE?

- [ ] HEARD GREAT THINGS
- [ ] IT LOOKED GOOD
- [ ] ONLY THING OPEN
- [ ] FORCED AGAINST WILL
- [ ] HUNGRY & DESPERATE
- [ ] WAS DRUNK

OTHER:

THE BEST THING(S) YOU ATE:

. . . .

THE WORST THING(S) YOU ATE:

. . . .

AMBIANCE
(1) (2) (3) (4) (5)

FOOD
(1) (2) (3) (4) (5)

SERVICE
(1) (2) (3) (4) (5)

THE ONE THING YOU'LL NEVER FORGET:

EAT HERE AGAIN?   YES [ ]   NO [ ]   IF DESPERATE [ ]

MOTHER APPROVED

NUMBER
129

NAME OF THE RESTAURANT

PSST: ADD THIS TO THE INDEX(ES) IN THE BACK SO YOU CAN FIND IT QUICKLY LATER

WHERE WAS IT LOCATED?

CITY: STATE/COUNTRY:

WHY DID YOU EAT HERE?

- [ ] HEARD GREAT THINGS
- [ ] IT LOOKED GOOD
- [ ] ONLY THING OPEN
- [ ] FORCED AGAINST WILL
- [ ] HUNGRY & DESPERATE
- [ ] WAS DRUNK

OTHER:

AMBIANCE
① ② ③ ④ ⑤

FOOD
① ② ③ ④ ⑤

SERVICE
① ② ③ ④ ⑤

THE BEST THING(S) YOU ATE:
. . . .

THE WORST THING(S) YOU ATE:
. . . .

THE ONE THING YOU'LL NEVER FORGET:

EAT HERE AGAIN? YES [ ] NO [ ] IF DESPERATE [ ]

MOTHER APPROVED

AKA: CHAINS

NAME OF THE RESTAURANT

NUMBER

130

PSST: ADD THIS TO THE INDEX(ES) IN THE BACK SO YOU CAN FIND IT QUICKLY LATER

WHERE WAS IT LOCATED?

CITY: STATE/COUNTRY:

WHY DID YOU EAT HERE?

- [ ] HEARD GREAT THINGS
- [ ] IT LOOKED GOOD
- [ ] ONLY THING OPEN
- [ ] FORCED AGAINST WILL
- [ ] HUNGRY & DESPERATE
- [ ] WAS DRUNK

OTHER:

THE BEST THING(S) YOU ATE:

. . . .

THE WORST THING(S) YOU ATE:

. . . .

AMBIANCE
(1) (2) (3) (4) (5)

FOOD
(1) (2) (3) (4) (5)

SERVICE
(1) (2) (3) (4) (5)

THE ONE THING YOU'LL NEVER FORGET:

EAT HERE AGAIN?   YES [ ]   NO [ ]   IF DESPERATE [ ]

NUMBER

131

NAME OF THE RESTAURANT

PSST: ADD THIS TO THE INDEX(ES) IN THE BACK SO YOU CAN FIND IT QUICKLY LATER

WHERE WAS IT LOCATED?

CITY: STATE/COUNTRY:

WHY DID YOU EAT HERE?

- [ ] HEARD GREAT THINGS
- [ ] IT LOOKED GOOD
- [ ] ONLY THING OPEN
- [ ] FORCED AGAINST WILL
- [ ] HUNGRY & DESPERATE
- [ ] WAS DRUNK

OTHER:

AMBIANCE
① ② ③ ④ ⑤

FOOD
① ② ③ ④ ⑤

SERVICE
① ② ③ ④ ⑤

THE BEST THING(S) YOU ATE:

. . . .

THE WORST THING(S) YOU ATE:

. . . .

THE ONE THING YOU'LL NEVER FORGET:

EAT HERE AGAIN?   YES [ ]   NO [ ]   IF DESPERATE [ ]

MOTHER APPROVED

AKA: CHAINS

NAME OF THE RESTAURANT

NUMBER

132

PSST: ADD THIS TO THE INDEX(ES) IN THE BACK SO YOU CAN FIND IT QUICKLY LATER

WHERE WAS IT LOCATED?

CITY: STATE/COUNTRY:

WHY DID YOU EAT HERE?

☐ HEARD GREAT THINGS   FORCED AGAINST WILL ☐

☐ IT LOOKED GOOD   HUNGRY & DESPERATE ☐

☐ ONLY THING OPEN   WAS DRUNK ☐

OTHER:

THE BEST THING(S) YOU ATE:

. . . .

AMBIANCE
① ② ③ ④ ⑤

FOOD
① ② ③ ④ ⑤

THE WORST THING(S) YOU ATE:

. . . .

SERVICE
① ② ③ ④ ⑤

THE ONE THING YOU'LL NEVER FORGET:

EAT HERE AGAIN?   YES ☐   NO ☐   IF DESPERATE ☐

NUMBER

133

NAME OF THE RESTAURANT

PSST: ADD THIS TO THE INDEX(ES) IN THE BACK SO YOU CAN FIND IT QUICKLY LATER

WHERE WAS IT LOCATED?

CITY: STATE/COUNTRY:

WHY DID YOU EAT HERE?

- [ ] HEARD GREAT THINGS
- [ ] IT LOOKED GOOD
- [ ] ONLY THING OPEN

FORCED AGAINST WILL [ ]
HUNGRY & DESPERATE [ ]
WAS DRUNK [ ]

OTHER:

AMBIANCE
① ② ③ ④ ⑤

FOOD
① ② ③ ④ ⑤

SERVICE
① ② ③ ④ ⑤

THE BEST THING(S) YOU ATE:

. . . .

THE WORST THING(S) YOU ATE:

. . . .

THE ONE THING YOU'LL NEVER FORGET:

EAT HERE AGAIN?   YES [ ]   NO [ ]   IF DESPERATE [ ]

NAME OF THE RESTAURANT

NUMBER

134

PSST: ADD THIS TO THE INDEX(ES) IN THE BACK SO YOU CAN FIND IT QUICKLY LATER

WHERE WAS IT LOCATED?

CITY: STATE/COUNTRY:

WHY DID YOU EAT HERE?

- [ ] HEARD GREAT THINGS
- [ ] IT LOOKED GOOD
- [ ] ONLY THING OPEN
- [ ] FORCED AGAINST WILL
- [ ] HUNGRY & DESPERATE
- [ ] WAS DRUNK

OTHER:

THE BEST THING(S) YOU ATE:

. . . .

THE WORST THING(S) YOU ATE:

. . . .

AMBIANCE
(1) (2) (3) (4) (5)

FOOD
(1) (2) (3) (4) (5)

SERVICE
(1) (2) (3) (4) (5)

THE ONE THING YOU'LL NEVER FORGET:

EAT HERE AGAIN?   YES [ ]   NO [ ]   IF DESPERATE [ ]

FRENCH FRIES

NATIONAL FRENCH FRY DAY IS THE 2ND FRIDAY IN JULY

PERFECT FOR	TERRIBLE FOR
☐ EATING VEGETABLES	SELF-RESTRAINT ☐
☐ DIPPING IN MILKSHAKES	HIGH BLOOD PRESSURE ☐

MCDONALD'S WAS ORIGINALLY FOUNDED AS A BARBECUE RESTAURANT IN 1940—BUT THEIR FRIES WERE STILL ON THAT VERY FIRST MENU, MAKING THEM THE ONLY SURVIVING ORIGINAL ITEM. MAYBE THAT'S WHY THEY'RE CONSISTENTLY RATED AS THE BEST FAST FOOD FRIES IN THE WORLD—OR MAYBE IT'S JUST NOSTALGIA.

FIND NOTABLES AT: KNOWN FOR

☐	FREDDY'S STEAKBURGERS	SHOESTRING FRIES
☐	ARBY'S	CURLY FRIES
☐	CHECKERS/RALLY'S	SEASONED FRIES
☐	CHICK-FIL-A	WAFFLE FRIES
☐	POPEYE'S CHICKEN	CAJUN FRIES
☐	IN-N-OUT	ANIMAL-STYLE FRIES
☐	TACO BELL	NACHO FRIES
☐	KENTUCKY FRIED CHICKEN	SECRET RECIPE FRIES
☐	WENDY'S	HOT & CRISPY FRIES
☐	RAISING CANE'S	CRINKLE-CUT FRIES
☐	WHATABURGER	FRIES W/ SPICY KETCHUP
☐	HARDEE'S/CARL'S JR	NATURAL-CUT FRIES

WRITE-IN CANDIDATES

MOTHER APPROVED

AKA: CHAINS

NAME OF THE RESTAURANT

NUMBER

135

PSST: ADD THIS TO THE INDEX(ES) IN THE BACK SO YOU CAN FIND IT QUICKLY LATER

WHERE WAS IT LOCATED?

CITY: STATE/COUNTRY:

WHY DID YOU EAT HERE?

- [ ] HEARD GREAT THINGS
- [ ] IT LOOKED GOOD
- [ ] ONLY THING OPEN
- [ ] FORCED AGAINST WILL
- [ ] HUNGRY & DESPERATE
- [ ] WAS DRUNK

OTHER:

THE BEST THING(S) YOU ATE:

. . . .

AMBIANCE
① ② ③ ④ ⑤

FOOD
① ② ③ ④ ⑤

THE WORST THING(S) YOU ATE:

. . . .

SERVICE
① ② ③ ④ ⑤

THE ONE THING YOU'LL NEVER FORGET:

EAT HERE AGAIN?   YES [ ]   NO [ ]   IF DESPERATE [ ]

MOTHER APPROVED

NUMBER

136

NAME OF THE RESTAURANT

PSST: ADD THIS TO THE INDEX(ES) IN THE BACK SO YOU CAN FIND IT QUICKLY LATER

WHERE WAS IT LOCATED?

CITY: STATE/COUNTRY:

WHY DID YOU EAT HERE?

- [ ] HEARD GREAT THINGS
- [ ] IT LOOKED GOOD
- [ ] ONLY THING OPEN
- [ ] FORCED AGAINST WILL
- [ ] HUNGRY & DESPERATE
- [ ] WAS DRUNK

OTHER:

AMBIANCE
① ② ③ ④ ⑤

FOOD
① ② ③ ④ ⑤

SERVICE
① ② ③ ④ ⑤

THE BEST THING(S) YOU ATE:
. . . .

THE WORST THING(S) YOU ATE:
. . . .

THE ONE THING YOU'LL NEVER FORGET:

EAT HERE AGAIN?   YES ☐   NO ☐   IF DESPERATE ☐

MOTHER APPROVED

AKA: CHAINS

NAME OF THE RESTAURANT

NUMBER

137

PSST: ADD THIS TO THE INDEX(ES) IN THE BACK SO YOU CAN FIND IT QUICKLY LATER

WHERE WAS IT LOCATED?

CITY: STATE/COUNTRY:

WHY DID YOU EAT HERE?

- [ ] HEARD GREAT THINGS
- [ ] IT LOOKED GOOD
- [ ] ONLY THING OPEN

- FORCED AGAINST WILL [ ]
- HUNGRY & DESPERATE [ ]
- WAS DRUNK [ ]

OTHER:

THE BEST THING(S) YOU ATE:

. . . .

THE WORST THING(S) YOU ATE:

. . . .

AMBIANCE
(1) (2) (3) (4) (5)

FOOD
(1) (2) (3) (4) (5)

SERVICE
(1) (2) (3) (4) (5)

THE ONE THING YOU'LL NEVER FORGET:

EAT HERE AGAIN?   YES [ ]   NO [ ]   IF DESPERATE [ ]

NUMBER

138

NAME OF THE RESTAURANT

PSST: ADD THIS TO THE INDEX(ES) IN THE BACK SO YOU CAN FIND IT QUICKLY LATER

WHERE WAS IT LOCATED?

CITY: STATE/COUNTRY:

WHY DID YOU EAT HERE?

- [ ] HEARD GREAT THINGS
- [ ] IT LOOKED GOOD
- [ ] ONLY THING OPEN

- [ ] FORCED AGAINST WILL
- [ ] HUNGRY & DESPERATE
- [ ] WAS DRUNK

OTHER:

AMBIANCE
(1) (2) (3) (4) (5)

FOOD
(1) (2) (3) (4) (5)

SERVICE
(1) (2) (3) (4) (5)

THE BEST THING(S) YOU ATE:

. . . .

THE WORST THING(S) YOU ATE:

. . . .

THE ONE THING YOU'LL NEVER FORGET:

EAT HERE AGAIN?   YES [ ]   NO [ ]   IF DESPERATE [ ]

MOTHER APPROVED

AKA: CHAINS

NAME OF THE RESTAURANT

NUMBER

139

PSST: ADD THIS TO THE INDEX(ES) IN THE BACK SO YOU CAN FIND IT QUICKLY LATER

WHERE WAS IT LOCATED?

CITY: STATE/COUNTRY:

WHY DID YOU EAT HERE?

- [ ] HEARD GREAT THINGS
- [ ] IT LOOKED GOOD
- [ ] ONLY THING OPEN
- [ ] FORCED AGAINST WILL
- [ ] HUNGRY & DESPERATE
- [ ] WAS DRUNK

OTHER:

THE BEST THING(S) YOU ATE:

. . . .

AMBIANCE
① ② ③ ④ ⑤

FOOD
① ② ③ ④ ⑤

THE WORST THING(S) YOU ATE:

. . . .

SERVICE
① ② ③ ④ ⑤

THE ONE THING YOU'LL NEVER FORGET:

EAT HERE AGAIN? YES [ ] NO [ ] IF DESPERATE [ ]

MOTHER APPROVED

NUMBER

140

NAME OF THE RESTAURANT

PSST: ADD THIS TO THE INDEX(ES) IN THE BACK SO YOU CAN FIND IT QUICKLY LATER

WHERE WAS IT LOCATED?

CITY: STATE/COUNTRY:

WHY DID YOU EAT HERE?

- [ ] HEARD GREAT THINGS
- [ ] IT LOOKED GOOD
- [ ] ONLY THING OPEN

- [ ] FORCED AGAINST WILL
- [ ] HUNGRY & DESPERATE
- [ ] WAS DRUNK

OTHER:

AMBIANCE
① ② ③ ④ ⑤

FOOD
① ② ③ ④ ⑤

SERVICE
① ② ③ ④ ⑤

THE BEST THING(S) YOU ATE:

. . . .

THE WORST THING(S) YOU ATE:

. . . .

THE ONE THING YOU'LL NEVER FORGET:

EAT HERE AGAIN?   YES [ ]   NO [ ]   IF DESPERATE [ ]

MOTHER APPROVED

NAME OF THE RESTAURANT

NUMBER

141

PSST: ADD THIS TO THE INDEX(ES) IN THE BACK SO YOU CAN FIND IT QUICKLY LATER

WHERE WAS IT LOCATED?

CITY: STATE/COUNTRY:

WHY DID YOU EAT HERE?

☐ HEARD GREAT THINGS   FORCED AGAINST WILL ☐
☐ IT LOOKED GOOD   HUNGRY & DESPERATE ☐
☐ ONLY THING OPEN   WAS DRUNK ☐

OTHER:

THE BEST THING(S) YOU ATE:

. . . .

AMBIANCE
① ② ③ ④ ⑤

FOOD
① ② ③ ④ ⑤

THE WORST THING(S) YOU ATE:

. . . .

SERVICE
① ② ③ ④ ⑤

THE ONE THING YOU'LL NEVER FORGET:

EAT HERE AGAIN?   YES ☐   NO ☐   IF DESPERATE ☐

A FEW MUST-TRYS

RESTAURANT	LOCATIONS
☐ TUPELO HONEY	NC, SC, TN, VA
☐ BIBIBOP	DC, IN, IL, KS, MO, MD, OH
☐ MODERN MARKET	AZ, IN, CO, TX
☐ RISE SOUTHERN BISCUITS	CA, FL, KS, MD, NC, TN
☐ &PIZZA	DC, MA, NJ, NY, PA, VA
☐ LION'S CHOICE	IL, KS, MO
☐ LUKE'S LOBSTER	DC, IL, MA, NY, PA
☐ COVER 3	TX
☐ ZIPPY'S	HI, NV
☐ LAZY DOG	CA, CO, FL, GA, IL, NV, TX, VA
☐ MAID-RITE	IA, IL, MN, MO, OH
☐ URBAN PLATES	CA
☐ PIADA STREET FOOD	OH, TX, IN, PA, KY, MN, MI
☐ FUKU	FL, MA, MD, NY, PA, TX
☐ BAREBURGER	NY, OH, PA
☐ DAT DOG	LA
☐ NAF NAF	FL, GA, IL, IN, MN, NJ, OH, PA, SC
☐ THE LITTLE BEET	CT, DC, NY, VA
☐ CURRY UP NOW	CA, CO, IN, GA, NJ, TX, UT
☐ SNOOZE	AZ, CA, CO, GA, KS, MO, NC, TX
☐ PDQ	FL, NC, NJ, NY, SC
☐ MENDOCINO FARMS	CA, TX
☐ PUNCH BOWL SOCIAL	CO, DC, FL, GA, IL, TX
☐ BIG JOHN'S STEAK & ONION	MI

WRITE-IN CANDIDATES

MOTHER APPROVED

NAME OF THE RESTAURANT

NUMBER

142

PSST: ADD THIS TO THE INDEX(ES) IN THE BACK SO YOU CAN FIND IT QUICKLY LATER

WHERE WAS IT LOCATED?

CITY: STATE/COUNTRY:

WHY DID YOU EAT HERE?

- [ ] HEARD GREAT THINGS
- [ ] IT LOOKED GOOD
- [ ] ONLY THING OPEN
- [ ] FORCED AGAINST WILL
- [ ] HUNGRY & DESPERATE
- [ ] WAS DRUNK

OTHER:

THE BEST THING(S) YOU ATE:

. . . .

THE WORST THING(S) YOU ATE:

. . . .

AMBIANCE
(1) (2) (3) (4) (5)

FOOD
(1) (2) (3) (4) (5)

SERVICE
(1) (2) (3) (4) (5)

THE ONE THING YOU'LL NEVER FORGET:

EAT HERE AGAIN?   YES [ ]   NO [ ]   IF DESPERATE [ ]

MOTHER APPROVED

NUMBER
143

NAME OF THE RESTAURANT

PSST: ADD THIS TO THE INDEX(ES) IN THE BACK SO YOU CAN FIND IT QUICKLY LATER

WHERE WAS IT LOCATED?

CITY: STATE/COUNTRY:

WHY DID YOU EAT HERE?

☐ HEARD GREAT THINGS   FORCED AGAINST WILL ☐
☐ IT LOOKED GOOD   HUNGRY & DESPERATE ☐
☐ ONLY THING OPEN   WAS DRUNK ☐

OTHER:

AMBIANCE
① ② ③ ④ ⑤

FOOD
① ② ③ ④ ⑤

SERVICE
① ② ③ ④ ⑤

THE BEST THING(S) YOU ATE:
. . . .

THE WORST THING(S) YOU ATE:
. . . .

THE ONE THING YOU'LL NEVER FORGET:

EAT HERE AGAIN?   YES ☐   NO ☐   IF DESPERATE ☐

MOTHER APPROVED

AKA: CHAINS

NAME OF THE RESTAURANT

NUMBER

144

PSST: ADD THIS TO THE INDEX(ES) IN THE BACK SO YOU CAN FIND IT QUICKLY LATER

WHERE WAS IT LOCATED?

CITY: STATE/COUNTRY:

WHY DID YOU EAT HERE?

- [ ] HEARD GREAT THINGS
- [ ] IT LOOKED GOOD
- [ ] ONLY THING OPEN
- [ ] FORCED AGAINST WILL
- [ ] HUNGRY & DESPERATE
- [ ] WAS DRUNK

OTHER:

THE BEST THING(S) YOU ATE:

. . . .

THE WORST THING(S) YOU ATE:

. . . .

AMBIANCE
(1) (2) (3) (4) (5)

FOOD
(1) (2) (3) (4) (5)

SERVICE
(1) (2) (3) (4) (5)

THE ONE THING YOU'LL NEVER FORGET:

EAT HERE AGAIN?   YES [ ]   NO [ ]   IF DESPERATE [ ]

MOTHER APPROVED

NUMBER

145

NAME OF THE RESTAURANT

PSST: ADD THIS TO THE INDEX(ES) IN THE BACK SO YOU CAN FIND IT QUICKLY LATER

WHERE WAS IT LOCATED?

CITY: STATE/COUNTRY:

WHY DID YOU EAT HERE?

- [ ] HEARD GREAT THINGS
- [ ] IT LOOKED GOOD
- [ ] ONLY THING OPEN
- [ ] FORCED AGAINST WILL
- [ ] HUNGRY & DESPERATE
- [ ] WAS DRUNK

OTHER:

AMBIANCE
(1) (2) (3) (4) (5)

FOOD
(1) (2) (3) (4) (5)

SERVICE
(1) (2) (3) (4) (5)

THE BEST THING(S) YOU ATE:

. . . .

THE WORST THING(S) YOU ATE:

. . . .

THE ONE THING YOU'LL NEVER FORGET:

EAT HERE AGAIN?   YES [ ]   NO [ ]   IF DESPERATE [ ]

MOTHER APPROVED

NAME OF THE RESTAURANT

NUMBER

146

PSST: ADD THIS TO THE INDEX(ES) IN THE BACK SO YOU CAN FIND IT QUICKLY LATER

WHERE WAS IT LOCATED?

CITY: STATE/COUNTRY:

WHY DID YOU EAT HERE?

☐ HEARD GREAT THINGS FORCED AGAINST WILL ☐
☐ IT LOOKED GOOD HUNGRY & DESPERATE ☐
☐ ONLY THING OPEN WAS DRUNK ☐

OTHER:

THE BEST THING(S) YOU ATE:

. . . .

THE WORST THING(S) YOU ATE:

. . . .

AMBIANCE
① ② ③ ④ ⑤

FOOD
① ② ③ ④ ⑤

SERVICE
① ② ③ ④ ⑤

THE ONE THING YOU'LL NEVER FORGET:

EAT HERE AGAIN? YES ☐ NO ☐ IF DESPERATE ☐

MOTHER APPROVED

NUMBER
147

NAME OF THE RESTAURANT

PSST: ADD THIS TO THE INDEX(ES) IN THE BACK SO YOU CAN FIND IT QUICKLY LATER

WHERE WAS IT LOCATED?

CITY: STATE/COUNTRY:

WHY DID YOU EAT HERE?

☐ HEARD GREAT THINGS FORCED AGAINST WILL ☐
☐ IT LOOKED GOOD HUNGRY & DESPERATE ☐
☐ ONLY THING OPEN WAS DRUNK ☐

OTHER:

AMBIANCE
① ② ③ ④ ⑤

FOOD
① ② ③ ④ ⑤

SERVICE
① ② ③ ④ ⑤

THE BEST THING(S) YOU ATE:
. . . .

THE WORST THING(S) YOU ATE:
. . . .

THE ONE THING YOU'LL NEVER FORGET:

EAT HERE AGAIN? YES ☐ NO ☐ IF DESPERATE ☐

MOTHER APPROVED

AKA: CHAINS

NAME OF THE RESTAURANT

NUMBER

148

PSST: ADD THIS TO THE INDEX(ES) IN THE BACK SO YOU CAN FIND IT QUICKLY LATER

WHERE WAS IT LOCATED?

CITY: STATE/COUNTRY:

WHY DID YOU EAT HERE?

- [ ] HEARD GREAT THINGS
- [ ] IT LOOKED GOOD
- [ ] ONLY THING OPEN
- [ ] FORCED AGAINST WILL
- [ ] HUNGRY & DESPERATE
- [ ] WAS DRUNK

OTHER:

THE BEST THING(S) YOU ATE:

. . . .

THE WORST THING(S) YOU ATE:

. . . .

AMBIANCE
(1) (2) (3) (4) (5)

FOOD
(1) (2) (3) (4) (5)

SERVICE
(1) (2) (3) (4) (5)

THE ONE THING YOU'LL NEVER FORGET:

EAT HERE AGAIN?   YES [ ]   NO [ ]   IF DESPERATE [ ]

TAKE A FOOD TOUR

COLUMBUS, OH

THE RESTAURANT TEST-MARKET CITY OF AMERICA

CHAINS FOUNDED IN COLUMBUS

- [ ] BUFFALO WILD WINGS
- [ ] WENDY'S
- [ ] MAX AND ERMA'S
- [ ] BOB EVAN'S

DUE TO ITS DIVERSITY, SIZE, AND AFFORDABLE COST OF REAL ESTATE, COLUMBUS HAS BECOME THE IDEAL CITY FOR SMALL RESTAURANT CHAINS TO EXPLORE EXPANSION OR TRY OUT NEW FOOD CONCEPTS—LIKE THESE.

RESTAURANT	KNOWN FOR
[ ] DAVE'S HOT CHICKEN	NASHVILLE HOT CHICKEN
[ ] ANOTHER BROKEN EGG	PANCAKES
[ ] BEERHEAD BAR & EATERY	BARBARIAN PRETZELS
[ ] THE ROOSEVELT ROOM	FINE COCKTAILS
[ ] MAPLE STREET BISCUIT CO.	BISCUITS
[ ] SAUCY BREW WORKS	SPECIALTY PIZZAS
[ ] SLURPING TURTLE	JAPANESE RAMEN
[ ] TRUE FOOD KITCHEN	HEALTH-CONSCIOUS MEALS
[ ] TORCHY'S TACOS	TRAILER PARK TACOS
[ ] ROOTS NATURAL KITCHEN	NATURAL FOOD
[ ] SONO WOOD FIRED	WOOD FIRED PIZZAS
[ ] SHEETZ	WISCONSIN CHEESE BITEZ
[ ] DEL-TACO	HABANERO CRISPY CHICKEN TACOS

WRITE-IN CANDIDATES

MOTHER APPROVED

AKA: CHAINS

NAME OF THE RESTAURANT

NUMBER

149

PSST: ADD THIS TO THE INDEX(ES) IN THE BACK SO YOU CAN FIND IT QUICKLY LATER

WHERE WAS IT LOCATED?

CITY: STATE/COUNTRY:

WHY DID YOU EAT HERE?

- [ ] HEARD GREAT THINGS
- [ ] IT LOOKED GOOD
- [ ] ONLY THING OPEN
- [ ] FORCED AGAINST WILL
- [ ] HUNGRY & DESPERATE
- [ ] WAS DRUNK

OTHER:

THE BEST THING(S) YOU ATE:

. . . .

THE WORST THING(S) YOU ATE:

. . . .

AMBIANCE
① ② ③ ④ ⑤

FOOD
① ② ③ ④ ⑤

SERVICE
① ② ③ ④ ⑤

THE ONE THING YOU'LL NEVER FORGET:

EAT HERE AGAIN? YES [ ] NO [ ] IF DESPERATE [ ]

MOTHER APPROVED

NUMBER
150

NAME OF THE RESTAURANT

PSST: ADD THIS TO THE INDEX(ES) IN THE BACK SO YOU CAN FIND IT QUICKLY LATER

WHERE WAS IT LOCATED?

CITY: STATE/COUNTRY:

WHY DID YOU EAT HERE?

- [ ] HEARD GREAT THINGS
- [ ] IT LOOKED GOOD
- [ ] ONLY THING OPEN
- [ ] FORCED AGAINST WILL
- [ ] HUNGRY & DESPERATE
- [ ] WAS DRUNK

OTHER:

AMBIANCE
① ② ③ ④ ⑤

FOOD
① ② ③ ④ ⑤

SERVICE
① ② ③ ④ ⑤

THE BEST THING(S) YOU ATE:

. . . .

THE WORST THING(S) YOU ATE:

. . . .

THE ONE THING YOU'LL NEVER FORGET:

EAT HERE AGAIN?   YES [ ]   NO [ ]   IF DESPERATE [ ]

HAD TO DRESS UP

HAD TO DRESS UP
AKA: ACTUAL FINE DINING

NAME OF THE RESTAURANT

NUMBER

151

PSST: ADD THIS TO THE INDEX(ES) IN THE BACK SO YOU CAN FIND IT QUICKLY LATER

WHERE WAS IT LOCATED?

CITY: STATE/COUNTRY:

WHY DID YOU EAT HERE?

☐ HEARD GREAT THINGS   FORCED AGAINST WILL ☐

☐ IT LOOKED GOOD   HUNGRY & DESPERATE ☐

☐ ONLY THING OPEN   WAS DRUNK ☐

OTHER:

THE BEST THING(S) YOU ATE:

. . . .

AMBIANCE
① ② ③ ④ ⑤

FOOD
① ② ③ ④ ⑤

THE WORST THING(S) YOU ATE:

. . . .

SERVICE
① ② ③ ④ ⑤

THE ONE THING YOU'LL NEVER FORGET:

EAT HERE AGAIN?   YES ☐   NO ☐   IF DESPERATE ☐

NUMBER
152

NAME OF THE RESTAURANT

PSST: ADD THIS TO THE INDEX(ES) IN THE BACK SO YOU CAN FIND IT QUICKLY LATER

WHERE WAS IT LOCATED?

CITY: STATE/COUNTRY:

WHY DID YOU EAT HERE?

- [ ] HEARD GREAT THINGS
- [ ] IT LOOKED GOOD
- [ ] ONLY THING OPEN
- [ ] FORCED AGAINST WILL
- [ ] HUNGRY & DESPERATE
- [ ] WAS DRUNK

OTHER:

AMBIANCE
① ② ③ ④ ⑤

FOOD
① ② ③ ④ ⑤

SERVICE
① ② ③ ④ ⑤

THE BEST THING(S) YOU ATE:
. . . .

THE WORST THING(S) YOU ATE:
. . . .

THE ONE THING YOU'LL NEVER FORGET:

EAT HERE AGAIN?   YES [ ]   NO [ ]   IF DESPERATE [ ]

HAD TO DRESS UP
AKA: ACTUAL FINE DINING

NAME OF THE RESTAURANT

NUMBER

153

PSST: ADD THIS TO THE INDEX(ES) IN THE BACK SO YOU CAN FIND IT QUICKLY LATER

WHERE WAS IT LOCATED?

CITY: STATE/COUNTRY:

WHY DID YOU EAT HERE?

- [ ] HEARD GREAT THINGS
- [ ] IT LOOKED GOOD
- [ ] ONLY THING OPEN
- [ ] FORCED AGAINST WILL
- [ ] HUNGRY & DESPERATE
- [ ] WAS DRUNK

OTHER:

THE BEST THING(S) YOU ATE:

. . . .

AMBIANCE
(1) (2) (3) (4) (5)

FOOD
(1) (2) (3) (4) (5)

THE WORST THING(S) YOU ATE:

. . . .

SERVICE
(1) (2) (3) (4) (5)

THE ONE THING YOU'LL NEVER FORGET:

EAT HERE AGAIN?   YES [ ]   NO [ ]   IF DESPERATE [ ]

HAD TO DRESS UP

NUMBER

154

NAME OF THE RESTAURANT

PSST: ADD THIS TO THE INDEX(ES) IN THE BACK SO YOU CAN FIND IT QUICKLY LATER

WHERE WAS IT LOCATED?

CITY: STATE/COUNTRY:

WHY DID YOU EAT HERE?

☐ HEARD GREAT THINGS   FORCED AGAINST WILL ☐

☐ IT LOOKED GOOD   HUNGRY & DESPERATE ☐

☐ ONLY THING OPEN   WAS DRUNK ☐

OTHER:

AMBIANCE

① ② ③ ④ ⑤

FOOD

① ② ③ ④ ⑤

SERVICE

① ② ③ ④ ⑤

THE BEST THING(S) YOU ATE:

. . . .

THE WORST THING(S) YOU ATE:

. . . .

THE ONE THING YOU'LL NEVER FORGET:

EAT HERE AGAIN?   YES ☐   NO ☐   IF DESPERATE ☐

HAD TO DRESS UP

AKA: ACTUAL FINE DINING

NAME OF THE RESTAURANT

NUMBER

155

PSST: ADD THIS TO THE INDEX(ES) IN THE BACK SO YOU CAN FIND IT QUICKLY LATER

WHERE WAS IT LOCATED?

CITY: STATE/COUNTRY:

WHY DID YOU EAT HERE?

- [ ] HEARD GREAT THINGS
- [ ] IT LOOKED GOOD
- [ ] ONLY THING OPEN
- [ ] FORCED AGAINST WILL
- [ ] HUNGRY & DESPERATE
- [ ] WAS DRUNK

OTHER:

THE BEST THING(S) YOU ATE:

. . . .

THE WORST THING(S) YOU ATE:

. . . .

AMBIANCE
(1) (2) (3) (4) (5)

FOOD
(1) (2) (3) (4) (5)

SERVICE
(1) (2) (3) (4) (5)

THE ONE THING YOU'LL NEVER FORGET:

EAT HERE AGAIN?   YES [ ]   NO [ ]   IF DESPERATE [ ]

HAD TO DRESS UP

NUMBER

156

NAME OF THE RESTAURANT

PSST: ADD THIS TO THE INDEX(ES) IN THE BACK SO YOU CAN FIND IT QUICKLY LATER

WHERE WAS IT LOCATED?

CITY: STATE/COUNTRY:

WHY DID YOU EAT HERE?

☐ HEARD GREAT THINGS   FORCED AGAINST WILL ☐

☐ IT LOOKED GOOD   HUNGRY & DESPERATE ☐

☐ ONLY THING OPEN   WAS DRUNK ☐

OTHER:

AMBIANCE

① ② ③ ④ ⑤

FOOD

① ② ③ ④ ⑤

SERVICE

① ② ③ ④ ⑤

THE BEST THING(S) YOU ATE:

. . . .

THE WORST THING(S) YOU ATE:

. . . .

THE ONE THING YOU'LL NEVER FORGET:

EAT HERE AGAIN?   YES ☐   NO ☐   IF DESPERATE ☐

HAD TO DRESS UP

AKA: ACTUAL FINE DINING

NAME OF THE RESTAURANT

NUMBER

157

PSST: ADD THIS TO THE INDEX(ES) IN THE BACK SO YOU CAN FIND IT QUICKLY LATER

WHERE WAS IT LOCATED?

CITY: STATE/COUNTRY:

WHY DID YOU EAT HERE?

☐ HEARD GREAT THINGS
☐ IT LOOKED GOOD
☐ ONLY THING OPEN

FORCED AGAINST WILL ☐
HUNGRY & DESPERATE ☐
WAS DRUNK ☐

OTHER:

THE BEST THING(S) YOU ATE:

. . . .

THE WORST THING(S) YOU ATE:

. . . .

AMBIANCE
① ② ③ ④ ⑤

FOOD
① ② ③ ④ ⑤

SERVICE
① ② ③ ④ ⑤

THE ONE THING YOU'LL NEVER FORGET:

EAT HERE AGAIN?   YES ☐   NO ☐   IF DESPERATE ☐

☐ BEEN THERE   KAYNE PRIME

1103 MCGAVOCK STREET, NASHVILLE, TN 37203

A FEW FAVORITES

PRIME STEAKS
① ② ③ ④ ⑤

☐ COTTON CANDY BACON

KANYNES SEEN
⓪ ① ② ③ ④

☐ POPCORN BUTTERED LOBSTER

☐ WAGYU FILET MIGNON

CALLING THIS PLACE A STEAKHOUSE IS AN ENORMOUS DISSERVICE TO HOW INCREDIBLE THIS RESTAURANT IS— BUT THIS IS PROBABLY ONE OF THE BEST STEAKHOUSES IN THE US. THE WAGYU FILET MIGNON WAS ONE OF THE BEST WE'VE EVER HAD—BUT IF WE ARE BEING HONEST, WE REALLY CAME HERE FOR THE HOUSE-MADE BACON TOPPED WITH A CLOUD OF COTTON CANDY. IT MELTS TOGETHER IN YOUR MOUTH FOR THE PERFECT SWEET & SALTY COMBINATION. WE STILL THINK ABOUT IT.

☐ BEEN THERE   PROVIDENCE

5955 MELROSE AVENUE, LOS ANGELES, CA 90038

A FEW FAVORITES

DOLLAR SIGNS
① ② ③ ④ ⑤

☐ THE UNI EGG

DOLLAR MENUS
⓪ ① ② ③ ④

☐ SALT-ROASTED SPOT PRAWNS

☐ RED FIFE SOURDOUGH BREAD

ENDING UP AT THIS PLACE WAS A WONDERFUL (ALBEIT PRICEY) ACCIDENT. ON A WHIM, WE ASKED OUR DRIVER FOR DINNER RECOMMENDATIONS WHILE WE WERE IN LOS ANGELES—AND WE ENDED UP HERE. OUR LOWLY GRAPHIC DESIGNER BANK ACCOUNTS WERE IN FOR A SHOCK WHEN WE GOT INSIDE, BUT WE WENT WITH IT—AND WE'RE SO GLAD WE DID. THIS RESTAURANT HAS 2 MICHELIN STARS FOR A REASON. I'D PAY GOOD MONEY JUST TO HAVE THE COMPLIMENTARY BREAD AGAIN—I'M NOT EVEN KIDDING.

HAD TO DRESS UP

AKA: ACTUAL FINE DINING

NAME OF THE RESTAURANT

NUMBER

158

PSST: ADD THIS TO THE INDEX(ES) IN THE BACK SO YOU CAN FIND IT QUICKLY LATER

WHERE WAS IT LOCATED?

CITY: STATE/COUNTRY:

WHY DID YOU EAT HERE?

- [ ] HEARD GREAT THINGS
- [ ] IT LOOKED GOOD
- [ ] ONLY THING OPEN
- [ ] FORCED AGAINST WILL
- [ ] HUNGRY & DESPERATE
- [ ] WAS DRUNK

OTHER:

THE BEST THING(S) YOU ATE:

. . . .

AMBIANCE
(1) (2) (3) (4) (5)

FOOD
(1) (2) (3) (4) (5)

THE WORST THING(S) YOU ATE:

. . . .

SERVICE
(1) (2) (3) (4) (5)

THE ONE THING YOU'LL NEVER FORGET:

EAT HERE AGAIN? YES [ ] NO [ ] IF DESPERATE [ ]

NUMBER

159

NAME OF THE RESTAURANT

PSST: ADD THIS TO THE INDEX(ES) IN THE BACK SO YOU CAN FIND IT QUICKLY LATER

WHERE WAS IT LOCATED?

CITY: STATE/COUNTRY:

WHY DID YOU EAT HERE?

- [ ] HEARD GREAT THINGS
- [ ] IT LOOKED GOOD
- [ ] ONLY THING OPEN
- [ ] FORCED AGAINST WILL
- [ ] HUNGRY & DESPERATE
- [ ] WAS DRUNK

OTHER:

AMBIANCE
① ② ③ ④ ⑤

FOOD
① ② ③ ④ ⑤

SERVICE
① ② ③ ④ ⑤

THE BEST THING(S) YOU ATE:
. . . .

THE WORST THING(S) YOU ATE:
. . . .

THE ONE THING YOU'LL NEVER FORGET:

EAT HERE AGAIN?   YES [ ]   NO [ ]   IF DESPERATE [ ]

HAD TO DRESS UP

NAME OF THE RESTAURANT

NUMBER

160

PSST: ADD THIS TO THE INDEX(ES) IN THE BACK SO YOU CAN FIND IT QUICKLY LATER

WHERE WAS IT LOCATED?

CITY: STATE/COUNTRY:

WHY DID YOU EAT HERE?

- [ ] HEARD GREAT THINGS
- [ ] IT LOOKED GOOD
- [ ] ONLY THING OPEN
- [ ] FORCED AGAINST WILL
- [ ] HUNGRY & DESPERATE
- [ ] WAS DRUNK

OTHER:

THE BEST THING(S) YOU ATE:

. . . .

THE WORST THING(S) YOU ATE:

. . . .

AMBIANCE
① ② ③ ④ ⑤

FOOD
① ② ③ ④ ⑤

SERVICE
① ② ③ ④ ⑤

THE ONE THING YOU'LL NEVER FORGET:

EAT HERE AGAIN?   YES [ ]   NO [ ]   IF DESPERATE [ ]

NUMBER

161

NAME OF THE RESTAURANT

PSST: ADD THIS TO THE INDEX(ES) IN THE BACK SO YOU CAN FIND IT QUICKLY LATER

WHERE WAS IT LOCATED?

CITY: STATE/COUNTRY:

WHY DID YOU EAT HERE?

- [ ] HEARD GREAT THINGS
- [ ] IT LOOKED GOOD
- [ ] ONLY THING OPEN
- [ ] FORCED AGAINST WILL
- [ ] HUNGRY & DESPERATE
- [ ] WAS DRUNK

OTHER:

AMBIANCE
(1) (2) (3) (4) (5)

FOOD
(1) (2) (3) (4) (5)

SERVICE
(1) (2) (3) (4) (5)

THE BEST THING(S) YOU ATE:

. . . .

THE WORST THING(S) YOU ATE:

. . . .

THE ONE THING YOU'LL NEVER FORGET:

EAT HERE AGAIN? YES [ ] NO [ ] IF DESPERATE [ ]

HAD TO DRESS UP

AKA: ACTUAL FINE DINING

NAME OF THE RESTAURANT

NUMBER

162

PSST: ADD THIS TO THE INDEX(ES) IN THE BACK SO YOU CAN FIND IT QUICKLY LATER

WHERE WAS IT LOCATED?

CITY: STATE/COUNTRY:

WHY DID YOU EAT HERE?

☐ HEARD GREAT THINGS   FORCED AGAINST WILL ☐
☐ IT LOOKED GOOD   HUNGRY & DESPERATE ☐
☐ ONLY THING OPEN   WAS DRUNK ☐

OTHER:

THE BEST THING(S) YOU ATE:

. . . .

THE WORST THING(S) YOU ATE:

. . . .

AMBIANCE
① ② ③ ④ ⑤

FOOD
① ② ③ ④ ⑤

SERVICE
① ② ③ ④ ⑤

THE ONE THING YOU'LL NEVER FORGET:

EAT HERE AGAIN?   YES ☐   NO ☐   IF DESPERATE ☐

NUMBER

163

NAME OF THE RESTAURANT

PSST: ADD THIS TO THE INDEX(ES) IN THE BACK SO YOU CAN FIND IT QUICKLY LATER

WHERE WAS IT LOCATED?

CITY: STATE/COUNTRY:

WHY DID YOU EAT HERE?

- [ ] HEARD GREAT THINGS
- [ ] IT LOOKED GOOD
- [ ] ONLY THING OPEN
- [ ] FORCED AGAINST WILL
- [ ] HUNGRY & DESPERATE
- [ ] WAS DRUNK

OTHER:

AMBIANCE
(1) (2) (3) (4) (5)

FOOD
(1) (2) (3) (4) (5)

SERVICE
(1) (2) (3) (4) (5)

THE BEST THING(S) YOU ATE:
. . . .

THE WORST THING(S) YOU ATE:
. . . .

THE ONE THING YOU'LL NEVER FORGET:

EAT HERE AGAIN?   YES [ ]   NO [ ]   IF DESPERATE [ ]

HAD TO DRESS UP

AKA: ACTUAL FINE DINING

NAME OF THE RESTAURANT

NUMBER

164

PSST: ADD THIS TO THE INDEX(ES) IN THE BACK SO YOU CAN FIND IT QUICKLY LATER

WHERE WAS IT LOCATED?

CITY: STATE/COUNTRY:

WHY DID YOU EAT HERE?

☐ HEARD GREAT THINGS   FORCED AGAINST WILL ☐

☐ IT LOOKED GOOD   HUNGRY & DESPERATE ☐

☐ ONLY THING OPEN   WAS DRUNK ☐

OTHER:

THE BEST THING(S) YOU ATE:

AMBIANCE
① ② ③ ④ ⑤

FOOD
① ② ③ ④ ⑤

THE WORST THING(S) YOU ATE:

SERVICE
① ② ③ ④ ⑤

THE ONE THING YOU'LL NEVER FORGET:

EAT HERE AGAIN?   YES ☐   NO ☐   IF DESPERATE ☐

FILET MIGNON

NATIONAL FILET MIGNON DAY IS ON AUGUST 13TH

PERFECT FOR	TERRIBLE FOR
☐ FEELING FANCY	FEELING FULL ☐
☐ IMPRESSING DATES	DEFLATING SAVINGS ☐

ALTHOUGH THE TERM IS FRENCH, THE PHRASE 'FILET MIGNON' WAS ORIGINALLY USED BY AMERICAN WRITER O. HENRY. IN HIS 1906 BOOK 'THE FOUR MILLION,' HE USED THE NAME SEVERAL TIMES—CONVEYING THE DISH AS A SYMBOL OF LUXURY AND ROMANCE. JUST DON'T ORDER ONE IN FRANCE—YOU'LL ACTUALLY GET PORK.

FIND NOTABLES AT: LOCATION

☐ BARCLAY PRIME	PHILADELPHIA, PA
☐ ST. ELMO STEAK HOUSE	INDIANAPOLIS, IN
☐ GALLAGHERS STEAKHOUSE	NEW YORK, NY
☐ BATEAU	SEATTLE, WA
☐ GOLDEN STEER STEAKHOUSE	LAS VEGAS, NV
☐ BERN'S STEAK HOUSE	TAMPA, FL
☐ KNIFE	DALLAS, TX
☐ BAVETTE'S BAR & BOEUF	CHICAGO, IL
☐ GAUCHO PARILLA ARGENTINA	PITTSBURGH, PA
☐ GUARD AND GRACE	HOUSTON, TX
☐ RINGSIDE STEAKHOUSE	PORTLAND, OR
☐ THE PRECINCT BY JEFF RUBY	CINCINNATI, OH

WRITE-IN CANDIDATES

HAD TO DRESS UP

AKA: ACTUAL FINE DINING

NAME OF THE RESTAURANT

NUMBER

165

PSST: ADD THIS TO THE INDEX(ES) IN THE BACK SO YOU CAN FIND IT QUICKLY LATER

WHERE WAS IT LOCATED?

CITY: STATE/COUNTRY:

WHY DID YOU EAT HERE?

- [ ] HEARD GREAT THINGS
- [ ] IT LOOKED GOOD
- [ ] ONLY THING OPEN
- [ ] FORCED AGAINST WILL
- [ ] HUNGRY & DESPERATE
- [ ] WAS DRUNK

OTHER:

THE BEST THING(S) YOU ATE:

. . . .

THE WORST THING(S) YOU ATE:

. . . .

AMBIANCE
(1) (2) (3) (4) (5)

FOOD
(1) (2) (3) (4) (5)

SERVICE
(1) (2) (3) (4) (5)

THE ONE THING YOU'LL NEVER FORGET:

EAT HERE AGAIN?   YES [ ]   NO [ ]   IF DESPERATE [ ]

NUMBER

166

NAME OF THE RESTAURANT

PSST: ADD THIS TO THE INDEX(ES) IN THE BACK SO YOU CAN FIND IT QUICKLY LATER

WHERE WAS IT LOCATED?

CITY: STATE/COUNTRY:

WHY DID YOU EAT HERE?

☐ HEARD GREAT THINGS ☐ FORCED AGAINST WILL

☐ IT LOOKED GOOD ☐ HUNGRY & DESPERATE

☐ ONLY THING OPEN ☐ WAS DRUNK

OTHER:

AMBIANCE

① ② ③ ④ ⑤

THE BEST THING(S) YOU ATE:

. . . .

FOOD

① ② ③ ④ ⑤

THE WORST THING(S) YOU ATE:

SERVICE

① ② ③ ④ ⑤

. . . .

THE ONE THING YOU'LL NEVER FORGET:

EAT HERE AGAIN? YES ☐ NO ☐ IF DESPERATE ☐

HAD TO DRESS UP

AKA: ACTUAL FINE DINING

NAME OF THE RESTAURANT

NUMBER

167

PSST: ADD THIS TO THE INDEX(ES) IN THE BACK SO YOU CAN FIND IT QUICKLY LATER

WHERE WAS IT LOCATED?

CITY: STATE/COUNTRY:

WHY DID YOU EAT HERE?

☐ HEARD GREAT THINGS   FORCED AGAINST WILL ☐

☐ IT LOOKED GOOD   HUNGRY & DESPERATE ☐

☐ ONLY THING OPEN   WAS DRUNK ☐

OTHER:

THE BEST THING(S) YOU ATE:

. . . .

AMBIANCE

① ② ③ ④ ⑤

FOOD

① ② ③ ④ ⑤

THE WORST THING(S) YOU ATE:

. . . .

SERVICE

① ② ③ ④ ⑤

THE ONE THING YOU'LL NEVER FORGET:

EAT HERE AGAIN?   YES ☐   NO ☐   IF DESPERATE ☐

HAD TO DRESS UP

NUMBER

168

NAME OF THE RESTAURANT

PSST: ADD THIS TO THE INDEX(ES) IN THE BACK SO YOU CAN FIND IT QUICKLY LATER

WHERE WAS IT LOCATED?

CITY: STATE/COUNTRY:

WHY DID YOU EAT HERE?

- [ ] HEARD GREAT THINGS
- [ ] IT LOOKED GOOD
- [ ] ONLY THING OPEN
- [ ] FORCED AGAINST WILL
- [ ] HUNGRY & DESPERATE
- [ ] WAS DRUNK

OTHER:

AMBIANCE
(1) (2) (3) (4) (5)

FOOD
(1) (2) (3) (4) (5)

SERVICE
(1) (2) (3) (4) (5)

THE BEST THING(S) YOU ATE:
. . . .

THE WORST THING(S) YOU ATE:
. . . .

THE ONE THING YOU'LL NEVER FORGET:

EAT HERE AGAIN?   YES [ ]   NO [ ]   IF DESPERATE [ ]

HAD TO DRESS UP

AKA: ACTUAL FINE DINING

NAME OF THE RESTAURANT

NUMBER

169

PSST: ADD THIS TO THE INDEX(ES) IN THE BACK SO YOU CAN FIND IT QUICKLY LATER

WHERE WAS IT LOCATED?

CITY: STATE/COUNTRY:

WHY DID YOU EAT HERE?

☐ HEARD GREAT THINGS   FORCED AGAINST WILL ☐

☐ IT LOOKED GOOD   HUNGRY & DESPERATE ☐

☐ ONLY THING OPEN   WAS DRUNK ☐

OTHER:

THE BEST THING(S) YOU ATE:

. . . .

AMBIANCE
① ② ③ ④ ⑤

FOOD
① ② ③ ④ ⑤

THE WORST THING(S) YOU ATE:

. . . .

SERVICE
① ② ③ ④ ⑤

THE ONE THING YOU'LL NEVER FORGET:

EAT HERE AGAIN?   YES ☐   NO ☐   IF DESPERATE ☐

HAD TO DRESS UP

NUMBER

170

NAME OF THE RESTAURANT

PSST: ADD THIS TO THE INDEX(ES) IN THE BACK SO YOU CAN FIND IT QUICKLY LATER

WHERE WAS IT LOCATED?

CITY: STATE/COUNTRY:

WHY DID YOU EAT HERE?

- [ ] HEARD GREAT THINGS
- [ ] IT LOOKED GOOD
- [ ] ONLY THING OPEN
- [ ] FORCED AGAINST WILL
- [ ] HUNGRY & DESPERATE
- [ ] WAS DRUNK

OTHER:

AMBIANCE
(1) (2) (3) (4) (5)

FOOD
(1) (2) (3) (4) (5)

SERVICE
(1) (2) (3) (4) (5)

THE BEST THING(S) YOU ATE:
. . . .

THE WORST THING(S) YOU ATE:
. . . .

THE ONE THING YOU'LL NEVER FORGET:

EAT HERE AGAIN?   YES [ ]   NO [ ]   IF DESPERATE [ ]

HAD TO DRESS UP

AKA: ACTUAL FINE DINING

NAME OF THE RESTAURANT

NUMBER

171

PSST: ADD THIS TO THE INDEX(ES) IN THE BACK SO YOU CAN FIND IT QUICKLY LATER

WHERE WAS IT LOCATED?

CITY: STATE/COUNTRY:

WHY DID YOU EAT HERE?

- [ ] HEARD GREAT THINGS
- [ ] IT LOOKED GOOD
- [ ] ONLY THING OPEN
- [ ] FORCED AGAINST WILL
- [ ] HUNGRY & DESPERATE
- [ ] WAS DRUNK

OTHER:

THE BEST THING(S) YOU ATE:

. . . .

THE WORST THING(S) YOU ATE:

. . . .

AMBIANCE
(1) (2) (3) (4) (5)

FOOD
(1) (2) (3) (4) (5)

SERVICE
(1) (2) (3) (4) (5)

THE ONE THING YOU'LL NEVER FORGET:

EAT HERE AGAIN?   YES [ ]   NO [ ]   IF DESPERATE [ ]

A FEW MUST-TRYS

RESTAURANT	LOCATION
☐ NOMA	COPENHAGEN, DENMARK
☐ THE KITCHEN RESTAURANT	SACRAMENTO, CA
☐ BAD ROMAN	NEW YORK, NY
☐ TRUST	SANTA ANA, CA
☐ THE FAT DUCK	BRAY, BERKSHIRE
☐ OXALIS	NEW YORK, NY
☐ CROW'S NEST	ANCHORAGE, AK
☐ LE FOU FROG	KANSAS CITY, MO
☐ MARCH	HOUSTON, TX
☐ TWO URBAN LICKS	ATLANTA, GA
☐ THE FRENCH LAUNDRY	YOUNTVILLE, CA
☐ CANLIS	SEATTLE, WA
☐ KADENCE	WINTER PARK, FL
☐ DIPDIPDIP TATSU-YA	AUSTIN, TX
☐ ELEVEN MADISON PARK	NEW YORK, NY
☐ CAFE MONARCH	SCOTTSDALE, AZ
☐ LE PIGEON	PORTLAND, OR
☐ VIDA	INDIANAPOLIS, IN
☐ CENTRAL	LIMA, PERU
☐ THE WHITNEY	DETROIT, MI
☐ ALINEA	CHICAGO, IL
☐ THE WALRUS & THE CARPENTER	SEATTLE, WA
☐ BACCHANALIA	ATLANTA, GA
☐ THE REFECTORY	COLUMBUS, OH

HAD TO DRESS UP

AKA: ACTUAL FINE DINING

NAME OF THE RESTAURANT

NUMBER

172

PSST: ADD THIS TO THE INDEX(ES) IN THE BACK SO YOU CAN FIND IT QUICKLY LATER

WHERE WAS IT LOCATED?

CITY: STATE/COUNTRY:

WHY DID YOU EAT HERE?

- [ ] HEARD GREAT THINGS
- [ ] IT LOOKED GOOD
- [ ] ONLY THING OPEN
- [ ] FORCED AGAINST WILL
- [ ] HUNGRY & DESPERATE
- [ ] WAS DRUNK

OTHER:

THE BEST THING(S) YOU ATE:

. . . .

THE WORST THING(S) YOU ATE:

. . . .

AMBIANCE
① ② ③ ④ ⑤

FOOD
① ② ③ ④ ⑤

SERVICE
① ② ③ ④ ⑤

THE ONE THING YOU'LL NEVER FORGET:

EAT HERE AGAIN? YES [ ] NO [ ] IF DESPERATE [ ]

NUMBER

173

NAME OF THE RESTAURANT

PSST: ADD THIS TO THE INDEX(ES) IN THE BACK SO YOU CAN FIND IT QUICKLY LATER

WHERE WAS IT LOCATED?

CITY: STATE/COUNTRY:

WHY DID YOU EAT HERE?

- [ ] HEARD GREAT THINGS
- [ ] IT LOOKED GOOD
- [ ] ONLY THING OPEN
- [ ] FORCED AGAINST WILL
- [ ] HUNGRY & DESPERATE
- [ ] WAS DRUNK

OTHER:

AMBIANCE
① ② ③ ④ ⑤

FOOD
① ② ③ ④ ⑤

SERVICE
① ② ③ ④ ⑤

THE BEST THING(S) YOU ATE:
. . . .

THE WORST THING(S) YOU ATE:
. . . .

THE ONE THING YOU'LL NEVER FORGET:

EAT HERE AGAIN?   YES [ ]   NO [ ]   IF DESPERATE [ ]

HAD TO DRESS UP

AKA: ACTUAL FINE DINING

NAME OF THE RESTAURANT

NUMBER

174

PSST: ADD THIS TO THE INDEX(ES) IN THE BACK SO YOU CAN FIND IT QUICKLY LATER

WHERE WAS IT LOCATED?

CITY: STATE/COUNTRY:

WHY DID YOU EAT HERE?

- [ ] HEARD GREAT THINGS
- [ ] IT LOOKED GOOD
- [ ] ONLY THING OPEN
- [ ] FORCED AGAINST WILL
- [ ] HUNGRY & DESPERATE
- [ ] WAS DRUNK

OTHER:

THE BEST THING(S) YOU ATE:

. . . .

THE WORST THING(S) YOU ATE:

. . . .

AMBIANCE
(1) (2) (3) (4) (5)

FOOD
(1) (2) (3) (4) (5)

SERVICE
(1) (2) (3) (4) (5)

THE ONE THING YOU'LL NEVER FORGET:

EAT HERE AGAIN?   YES [ ]   NO [ ]   IF DESPERATE [ ]

NUMBER

175

NAME OF THE RESTAURANT

PSST: ADD THIS TO THE INDEX(ES) IN THE BACK SO YOU CAN FIND IT QUICKLY LATER

WHERE WAS IT LOCATED?

CITY: STATE/COUNTRY:

WHY DID YOU EAT HERE?

- [ ] HEARD GREAT THINGS
- [ ] IT LOOKED GOOD
- [ ] ONLY THING OPEN
- [ ] FORCED AGAINST WILL
- [ ] HUNGRY & DESPERATE
- [ ] WAS DRUNK

OTHER:

AMBIANCE
(1)(2)(3)(4)(5)

FOOD
(1)(2)(3)(4)(5)

SERVICE
(1)(2)(3)(4)(5)

THE BEST THING(S) YOU ATE:

. . . .

THE WORST THING(S) YOU ATE:

. . . .

THE ONE THING YOU'LL NEVER FORGET:

EAT HERE AGAIN?   YES [ ]   NO [ ]   IF DESPERATE [ ]

HAD TO DRESS UP

AKA: ACTUAL FINE DINING

NAME OF THE RESTAURANT

NUMBER

176

PSST: ADD THIS TO THE INDEX(ES) IN THE BACK SO YOU CAN FIND IT QUICKLY LATER

WHERE WAS IT LOCATED?

CITY: STATE/COUNTRY:

WHY DID YOU EAT HERE?

- [ ] HEARD GREAT THINGS
- [ ] IT LOOKED GOOD
- [ ] ONLY THING OPEN
- [ ] FORCED AGAINST WILL
- [ ] HUNGRY & DESPERATE
- [ ] WAS DRUNK

OTHER:

THE BEST THING(S) YOU ATE:

. . . .

THE WORST THING(S) YOU ATE:

. . . .

AMBIANCE
(1) (2) (3) (4) (5)

FOOD
(1) (2) (3) (4) (5)

SERVICE
(1) (2) (3) (4) (5)

THE ONE THING YOU'LL NEVER FORGET:

EAT HERE AGAIN?   YES [ ]   NO [ ]   IF DESPERATE [ ]

HAD TO DRESS UP

NUMBER

177

NAME OF THE RESTAURANT

PSST: ADD THIS TO THE INDEX(ES) IN THE BACK SO YOU CAN FIND IT QUICKLY LATER

WHERE WAS IT LOCATED?

CITY: STATE/COUNTRY:

WHY DID YOU EAT HERE?

- [ ] HEARD GREAT THINGS
- [ ] IT LOOKED GOOD
- [ ] ONLY THING OPEN
- [ ] FORCED AGAINST WILL
- [ ] HUNGRY & DESPERATE
- [ ] WAS DRUNK

OTHER:

AMBIANCE
(1) (2) (3) (4) (5)

FOOD
(1) (2) (3) (4) (5)

SERVICE
(1) (2) (3) (4) (5)

THE BEST THING(S) YOU ATE:
. . . .

THE WORST THING(S) YOU ATE:
. . . .

THE ONE THING YOU'LL NEVER FORGET:

EAT HERE AGAIN?   YES [ ]   NO [ ]   IF DESPERATE [ ]

HAD TO DRESS UP

AKA: ACTUAL FINE DINING

NAME OF THE RESTAURANT

NUMBER

178

PSST: ADD THIS TO THE INDEX(ES) IN THE BACK SO YOU CAN FIND IT QUICKLY LATER

WHERE WAS IT LOCATED?

CITY: STATE/COUNTRY:

WHY DID YOU EAT HERE?

- [ ] HEARD GREAT THINGS
- [ ] IT LOOKED GOOD
- [ ] ONLY THING OPEN
- [ ] FORCED AGAINST WILL
- [ ] HUNGRY & DESPERATE
- [ ] WAS DRUNK

OTHER:

THE BEST THING(S) YOU ATE:

. . . .

THE WORST THING(S) YOU ATE:

. . . .

AMBIANCE
(1) (2) (3) (4) (5)

FOOD
(1) (2) (3) (4) (5)

SERVICE
(1) (2) (3) (4) (5)

THE ONE THING YOU'LL NEVER FORGET:

EAT HERE AGAIN?   YES [ ]   NO [ ]   IF DESPERATE [ ]

TAKE A FOOD TOUR

SAN FRANCISCO, CA

HAS 31 MICHELIN-STARRED RESTAURANTS (2022)

BEST DISTRICTS FOR FINE DINING

- [ ] UNION SQUARE
- [ ] SOUTH OF MARKET (SOMA)
- [ ] FINANCIAL DISTRICT
- [ ] THE MISSION

WITH NEARLY 4,000 PLACES TO EAT AT, SAN FRANCISCO HAS MORE DINING SPOTS PER CAPITA THAN ANY OTHER MAJOR CITY IN THE UNITED STATES. THAT IS BASICALLY ONE RESTAURANT FOR EVERY 205 PEOPLE.

RESTAURANT	CUISINE
[ ] ATELIER CRENN	FRENCH
[ ] BENU	CONTEMPORARY AMERICAN
[ ] MOURAD	MOROCCAN
[ ] SAISON	WOOD-FIRED NEW AMERICAN
[ ] NISEI	CONTEMPORARY JAPANESE
[ ] FRIENDS ONLY	OMAKASE
[ ] LAZY BEAR	CONTEMPORARY AMERICAN
[ ] NIKU STEAKHOUSE	JAPANESE-AMERICAN
[ ] BIRDSONG	PACIFIC NORTHWEST
[ ] APHOTIC	UPSCALE SEAFOOD
[ ] CALIFORNIOS	CONTEMPORARY MEXICAN
[ ] NIGHTBIRD	LOCALLY SEASONAL
[ ] QUINCE	CALIFORNIAN

WRITE-IN CANDIDATES

HAD TO DRESS UP

AKA: ACTUAL FINE DINING

NAME OF THE RESTAURANT

NUMBER

179

PSST: ADD THIS TO THE INDEX(ES) IN THE BACK SO YOU CAN FIND IT QUICKLY LATER

WHERE WAS IT LOCATED?

CITY:

STATE/COUNTRY:

WHY DID YOU EAT HERE?

☐ HEARD GREAT THINGS

☐ IT LOOKED GOOD

☐ ONLY THING OPEN

FORCED AGAINST WILL ☐

HUNGRY & DESPERATE ☐

WAS DRUNK ☐

OTHER:

THE BEST THING(S) YOU ATE:

. . . .

THE WORST THING(S) YOU ATE:

. . . .

AMBIANCE
① ② ③ ④ ⑤

FOOD
① ② ③ ④ ⑤

SERVICE
① ② ③ ④ ⑤

THE ONE THING YOU'LL NEVER FORGET:

EAT HERE AGAIN?   YES ☐   NO ☐   IF DESPERATE ☐

HAD TO DRESS UP

NUMBER

180

NAME OF THE RESTAURANT

PSST: ADD THIS TO THE INDEX(ES) IN THE BACK SO YOU CAN FIND IT QUICKLY LATER

WHERE WAS IT LOCATED?

CITY: STATE/COUNTRY:

WHY DID YOU EAT HERE?

- [ ] HEARD GREAT THINGS
- [ ] IT LOOKED GOOD
- [ ] ONLY THING OPEN
- [ ] FORCED AGAINST WILL
- [ ] HUNGRY & DESPERATE
- [ ] WAS DRUNK

OTHER:

AMBIANCE
① ② ③ ④ ⑤

FOOD
① ② ③ ④ ⑤

SERVICE
① ② ③ ④ ⑤

THE BEST THING(S) YOU ATE:

. . . .

THE WORST THING(S) YOU ATE:

. . . .

THE ONE THING YOU'LL NEVER FORGET:

EAT HERE AGAIN?   YES [ ]   NO [ ]   IF DESPERATE [ ]

LIQUID ASSETS

LIQUID ASSETS

AKA: BARS & SPEAKEASIES

NAME OF THE BAR

NUMBER

181

PSST: ADD THIS TO THE INDEX(ES) IN THE BACK SO YOU CAN FIND IT QUICKLY LATER

WHERE WAS IT LOCATED?

CITY: STATE/COUNTRY:

WHY DID YOU COME HERE?

- [ ] HEARD GREAT THINGS
- [ ] IT LOOKED GOOD
- [ ] ONLY THING OPEN

- [ ] FORCED AGAINST WILL
- [ ] KINDA DESPERATE
- [ ] WAS (ALREADY) DRUNK

OTHER:

THE BEST THING(S) YOU HAD:

. . . .

THE WORST THING(S) YOU HAD:

. . . .

AMBIANCE
(1) (2) (3) (4) (5)

DRINKS
(1) (2) (3) (4) (5)

SERVICE
(1) (2) (3) (4) (5)

THE ONE THING YOU'LL NEVER FORGET:

COME HERE AGAIN?   YES [ ]   NO [ ]   IF DESPERATE [ ]

LIQUID ASSETS

NUMBER

182

NAME OF THE BAR

PSST: ADD THIS TO THE INDEX(ES) IN THE BACK SO YOU CAN FIND IT QUICKLY LATER

WHERE WAS IT LOCATED?

CITY: STATE/COUNTRY:

WHY DID YOU COME HERE?

- [ ] HEARD GREAT THINGS
- [ ] IT LOOKED GOOD
- [ ] ONLY THING OPEN

- FORCED AGAINST WILL [ ]
- KINDA DESPERATE [ ]
- WAS (ALREADY) DRUNK [ ]

OTHER:

AMBIANCE
① ② ③ ④ ⑤

DRINKS
① ② ③ ④ ⑤

SERVICE
① ② ③ ④ ⑤

THE BEST THING(S) YOU HAD:
. . . .

THE WORST THING(S) YOU HAD:
. . . .

THE ONE THING YOU'LL NEVER FORGET:

COME HERE AGAIN?   YES [ ]   NO [ ]   IF DESPERATE [ ]

LIQUID ASSETS

AKA: BARS & SPEAKEASIES

NAME OF THE BAR

NUMBER

183

PSST: ADD THIS TO THE INDEX(ES) IN THE BACK SO YOU CAN FIND IT QUICKLY LATER

WHERE WAS IT LOCATED?

CITY: STATE/COUNTRY:

WHY DID YOU COME HERE?

- [ ] HEARD GREAT THINGS
- [ ] IT LOOKED GOOD
- [ ] ONLY THING OPEN

- FORCED AGAINST WILL [ ]
- KINDA DESPERATE [ ]
- WAS (ALREADY) DRUNK [ ]

OTHER:

THE BEST THING(S) YOU HAD:

. . . .

THE WORST THING(S) YOU HAD:

. . . .

AMBIANCE
① ② ③ ④ ⑤

DRINKS
① ② ③ ④ ⑤

SERVICE
① ② ③ ④ ⑤

THE ONE THING YOU'LL NEVER FORGET:

COME HERE AGAIN?   YES [ ]   NO [ ]   IF DESPERATE [ ]

LIQUID ASSETS

NUMBER

184

NAME OF THE BAR

PSST: ADD THIS TO THE INDEX(ES) IN THE BACK SO YOU CAN FIND IT QUICKLY LATER

WHERE WAS IT LOCATED?

CITY: STATE/COUNTRY:

WHY DID YOU COME HERE?

☐ HEARD GREAT THINGS   FORCED AGAINST WILL ☐
☐ IT LOOKED GOOD   KINDA DESPERATE ☐
☐ ONLY THING OPEN   WAS (ALREADY) DRUNK ☐

OTHER:

AMBIANCE
① ② ③ ④ ⑤

DRINKS
① ② ③ ④ ⑤

SERVICE
① ② ③ ④ ⑤

THE BEST THING(S) YOU HAD:

. . . .

THE WORST THING(S) YOU HAD:

. . . .

THE ONE THING YOU'LL NEVER FORGET:

COME HERE AGAIN?   YES ☐   NO ☐   IF DESPERATE ☐

LIQUID ASSETS

AKA: BARS & SPEAKEASIES

NAME OF THE BAR

NUMBER

185

PSST: ADD THIS TO THE INDEX(ES) IN THE BACK SO YOU CAN FIND IT QUICKLY LATER

WHERE WAS IT LOCATED?

CITY: STATE/COUNTRY:

WHY DID YOU COME HERE?

- [ ] HEARD GREAT THINGS
- [ ] IT LOOKED GOOD
- [ ] ONLY THING OPEN
- [ ] FORCED AGAINST WILL
- [ ] KINDA DESPERATE
- [ ] WAS (ALREADY) DRUNK

OTHER:

THE BEST THING(S) YOU HAD:

. . . .

THE WORST THING(S) YOU HAD:

. . . .

AMBIANCE
(1)(2)(3)(4)(5)

DRINKS
(1)(2)(3)(4)(5)

SERVICE
(1)(2)(3)(4)(5)

THE ONE THING YOU'LL NEVER FORGET:

COME HERE AGAIN?   YES [ ]   NO [ ]   IF DESPERATE [ ]

LIQUID ASSETS

NUMBER

186

NAME OF THE BAR

PSST: ADD THIS TO THE INDEX(ES) IN THE BACK SO YOU CAN FIND IT QUICKLY LATER

WHERE WAS IT LOCATED?

CITY: STATE/COUNTRY:

WHY DID YOU COME HERE?

- [ ] HEARD GREAT THINGS
- [ ] IT LOOKED GOOD
- [ ] ONLY THING OPEN
- [ ] FORCED AGAINST WILL
- [ ] KINDA DESPERATE
- [ ] WAS (ALREADY) DRUNK

OTHER:

AMBIANCE
① ② ③ ④ ⑤

DRINKS
① ② ③ ④ ⑤

SERVICE
① ② ③ ④ ⑤

THE BEST THING(S) YOU HAD:
. . . .

THE WORST THING(S) YOU HAD:
. . . .

THE ONE THING YOU'LL NEVER FORGET:

COME HERE AGAIN? YES [ ] NO [ ] IF DESPERATE [ ]

LIQUID ASSETS

AKA: BARS & SPEAKEASIES

NAME OF THE BAR

NUMBER

187

PSST: ADD THIS TO THE INDEX(ES) IN THE BACK SO YOU CAN FIND IT QUICKLY LATER

WHERE WAS IT LOCATED?

CITY: STATE/COUNTRY:

WHY DID YOU COME HERE?

- [ ] HEARD GREAT THINGS
- [ ] IT LOOKED GOOD
- [ ] ONLY THING OPEN

- [ ] FORCED AGAINST WILL
- [ ] KINDA DESPERATE
- [ ] WAS (ALREADY) DRUNK

OTHER:

THE BEST THING(S) YOU HAD:

. . . .

THE WORST THING(S) YOU HAD:

. . . .

AMBIANCE
(1) (2) (3) (4) (5)

DRINKS
(1) (2) (3) (4) (5)

SERVICE
(1) (2) (3) (4) (5)

THE ONE THING YOU'LL NEVER FORGET:

COME HERE AGAIN?   YES [ ]   NO [ ]   IF DESPERATE [ ]

OUR FAVORITES

☐ BEEN THERE

HOLD FAST

364 WEST 46TH STREET, NEW YORK, NY 10036

A FEW FAVORITES

☐ DEVILED EGGS (W/ BACON)

☐ SLOW-COOKED PORK FRIES

☐ BEER CHEESE (W/ CHIPS)

LOCATION
① ② ③ ④ ⑤

ADORATION
① ② ③ ④ ⑤

WE HAVE ONE RULE WHEN WE VISIT NEW YORK—AVOID TIMES SQUARE AT ALL COSTS. HOWEVER, WE MAKE ONE EXCEPTION, AND THAT'S TO VISIT THIS PLACE. IT'S IN THE BASEMENT OF A BROWNSTONE—DOWN THE STREET FROM THE BROADWAY THEATERS. WE'VE BEEN COMING HERE FOR YEARS. IN FACT, THE NIGHT WE STARTED THIS BRAND WE CAME HERE TO CELEBRATE. IT'S SMALL, SO GRAB SEATS AT THE BAR. WATCH THE BOB ROSS RERUNS PLAYING ON THE TV & EAT DEVILED EGGS—JUST LIKE US.

☐ BEEN THERE

TOWER TAVERN

401 EAST 31ST STREET, KANSAS CITY, MO 64108

A FEW FAVORITES

☐ ITALIAN COMBO PIZZA

☐ CHARRED WINGS

☐ A SIDE OF FRIES (W/ RANCH)

SPORTS ON MUTE
① ② ③ ④ ⑤

WORKING JUKEBOX
① ② ③ ④ ⑤

IF WE HAD OUR OWN 'CHEERS' BAR, THIS WOULD BE IT. DOES EVERYONE KNOW OUR NAMES? PROBABLY NOT—BUT THEY SURE AS HELL ALL KNOW OUR DRINKS. WE HAVE, ON OCCASION, HAD THEM WAITING FOR US BEFORE WE EVEN GET IN THE DOOR. THE WEIRD THING IS, IT'S A SPORTS BAR—AND WE DON'T EVEN WATCH SPORTS. LIKE, AT ALL. SO WHY IS THIS OUR GO-TO PLACE? WELL, THE FOOD (ALL OF IT) IS A HIDDEN GEM IN KANSAS CITY— AND SO ARE THE BARTENDERS. TELL NICK WE SAID HI.

LIQUID ASSETS

AKA: BARS & SPEAKEASIES

NAME OF THE BAR

NUMBER

188

PSST: ADD THIS TO THE INDEX(ES) IN THE BACK SO YOU CAN FIND IT QUICKLY LATER

WHERE WAS IT LOCATED?

CITY: STATE/COUNTRY:

WHY DID YOU COME HERE?

- [ ] HEARD GREAT THINGS
- [ ] IT LOOKED GOOD
- [ ] ONLY THING OPEN
- [ ] FORCED AGAINST WILL
- [ ] KINDA DESPERATE
- [ ] WAS (ALREADY) DRUNK

OTHER:

THE BEST THING(S) YOU HAD:

. . . .

AMBIANCE

(1) (2) (3) (4) (5)

DRINKS

(1) (2) (3) (4) (5)

THE WORST THING(S) YOU HAD:

. . . .

SERVICE

(1) (2) (3) (4) (5)

THE ONE THING YOU'LL NEVER FORGET:

COME HERE AGAIN?   YES [ ]   NO [ ]   IF DESPERATE [ ]

LIQUID ASSETS

NUMBER

189

NAME OF THE BAR

PSST: ADD THIS TO THE INDEX(ES) IN THE BACK SO YOU CAN FIND IT QUICKLY LATER

WHERE WAS IT LOCATED?

CITY: STATE/COUNTRY:

WHY DID YOU COME HERE?

- [ ] HEARD GREAT THINGS
- [ ] IT LOOKED GOOD
- [ ] ONLY THING OPEN

- [ ] FORCED AGAINST WILL
- [ ] KINDA DESPERATE
- [ ] WAS (ALREADY) DRUNK

OTHER:

AMBIANCE
① ② ③ ④ ⑤

DRINKS
① ② ③ ④ ⑤

SERVICE
① ② ③ ④ ⑤

THE BEST THING(S) YOU HAD:
. . . .

THE WORST THING(S) YOU HAD:
. . . .

THE ONE THING YOU'LL NEVER FORGET:

COME HERE AGAIN?   YES [ ]   NO [ ]   IF DESPERATE [ ]

LIQUID ASSETS

AKA: BARS & SPEAKEASIES

NAME OF THE BAR

NUMBER

190

PSST: ADD THIS TO THE INDEX(ES) IN THE BACK SO YOU CAN FIND IT QUICKLY LATER

WHERE WAS IT LOCATED?

CITY: STATE/COUNTRY:

WHY DID YOU COME HERE?

- [ ] HEARD GREAT THINGS
- [ ] IT LOOKED GOOD
- [ ] ONLY THING OPEN

- FORCED AGAINST WILL [ ]
- KINDA DESPERATE [ ]
- WAS (ALREADY) DRUNK [ ]

OTHER:

THE BEST THING(S) YOU HAD:

. . . .

THE WORST THING(S) YOU HAD:

. . . .

AMBIANCE
① ② ③ ④ ⑤

DRINKS
① ② ③ ④ ⑤

SERVICE
① ② ③ ④ ⑤

THE ONE THING YOU'LL NEVER FORGET:

COME HERE AGAIN?   YES [ ]   NO [ ]   IF DESPERATE [ ]

NUMBER

191

NAME OF THE BAR

PSST: ADD THIS TO THE INDEX(ES) IN THE BACK SO YOU CAN FIND IT QUICKLY LATER

WHERE WAS IT LOCATED?

CITY: STATE/COUNTRY:

WHY DID YOU COME HERE?

- [ ] HEARD GREAT THINGS
- [ ] IT LOOKED GOOD
- [ ] ONLY THING OPEN
- [ ] FORCED AGAINST WILL
- [ ] KINDA DESPERATE
- [ ] WAS (ALREADY) DRUNK

OTHER:

AMBIANCE
① ② ③ ④ ⑤

DRINKS
① ② ③ ④ ⑤

SERVICE
① ② ③ ④ ⑤

THE BEST THING(S) YOU HAD:
. . . .

THE WORST THING(S) YOU HAD:
. . . .

THE ONE THING YOU'LL NEVER FORGET:

COME HERE AGAIN?   YES [ ]   NO [ ]   IF DESPERATE [ ]

LIQUID ASSETS

AKA: BARS & SPEAKEASIES

NAME OF THE BAR

NUMBER

192

PSST: ADD THIS TO THE INDEX(ES) IN THE BACK SO YOU CAN FIND IT QUICKLY LATER

WHERE WAS IT LOCATED?

CITY: STATE/COUNTRY:

WHY DID YOU COME HERE?

- [ ] HEARD GREAT THINGS
- [ ] IT LOOKED GOOD
- [ ] ONLY THING OPEN
- [ ] FORCED AGAINST WILL
- [ ] KINDA DESPERATE
- [ ] WAS (ALREADY) DRUNK

OTHER:

THE BEST THING(S) YOU HAD:

. . . .

THE WORST THING(S) YOU HAD:

. . . .

AMBIANCE
① ② ③ ④ ⑤

DRINKS
① ② ③ ④ ⑤

SERVICE
① ② ③ ④ ⑤

THE ONE THING YOU'LL NEVER FORGET:

COME HERE AGAIN?   YES [ ]   NO [ ]   IF DESPERATE [ ]

LIQUID ASSETS

NUMBER

193

NAME OF THE BAR

PSST: ADD THIS TO THE INDEX(ES) IN THE BACK SO YOU CAN FIND IT QUICKLY LATER

WHERE WAS IT LOCATED?

CITY: STATE/COUNTRY:

WHY DID YOU COME HERE?

☐ HEARD GREAT THINGS   FORCED AGAINST WILL ☐

☐ IT LOOKED GOOD   KINDA DESPERATE ☐

☐ ONLY THING OPEN   WAS (ALREADY) DRUNK ☐

OTHER:

AMBIANCE
① ② ③ ④ ⑤

DRINKS
① ② ③ ④ ⑤

SERVICE
① ② ③ ④ ⑤

THE BEST THING(S) YOU HAD:

. . . .

THE WORST THING(S) YOU HAD:

. . . .

THE ONE THING YOU'LL NEVER FORGET:

COME HERE AGAIN?   YES ☐   NO ☐   IF DESPERATE ☐

LIQUID ASSETS

AKA: BARS & SPEAKEASIES

NAME OF THE BAR

NUMBER

194

PSST: ADD THIS TO THE INDEX(ES) IN THE BACK SO YOU CAN FIND IT QUICKLY LATER

WHERE WAS IT LOCATED?

CITY: STATE/COUNTRY:

WHY DID YOU COME HERE?

☐ HEARD GREAT THINGS   FORCED AGAINST WILL ☐

☐ IT LOOKED GOOD   KINDA DESPERATE ☐

☐ ONLY THING OPEN   WAS (ALREADY) DRUNK ☐

OTHER:

THE BEST THING(S) YOU HAD:

. . . .

AMBIANCE
① ② ③ ④ ⑤

DRINKS
① ② ③ ④ ⑤

THE WORST THING(S) YOU HAD:

. . . .

SERVICE
① ② ③ ④ ⑤

THE ONE THING YOU'LL NEVER FORGET:

COME HERE AGAIN?   YES ☐   NO ☐   IF DESPERATE ☐

BUFFALO WINGS

NATIONAL CHICKEN WING DAY IS ON JULY 29TH

PERFECT FOR	TERRIBLE FOR
☐ STAINING EVERYTHING	WEDDING RECEPTIONS ☐
☐ WEARING ORANGE	WEARING WHITE ☐

THE BUFFALO WING WAS (ALLEGEDLY) FIRST INVENTED IN 1964 AT THE 'ANCHOR BAR' IN BUFFALO, NY, WHEN THE OWNER OF THE BAR, TERESSA BELLISSIMO, FRIED UP THE CHICKEN INTENDED FOR SOUP STOCK TO SERVE AS A TREAT TO A LATE-NIGHT CROWD. THE BAR IS STILL THERE—SO GET SOME WHERE IT (LIKELY) ALL STARTED.

FIND NOTABLES AT: LOCATION

☐	JIMMIE KRAMER'S PEANUT BAR	READING, PA
☐	BUFFALO JOE'S	EVANSTON, IL
☐	JAKE MELNICK'S CORNER TAP	CHICAGO, IL
☐	J. TIMOTHY'S TAVERNE	PLAINVILLE, CT
☐	THE PEANUT	KANSAS CITY, MO
☐	LEGEND LARRY'S	GREEN BAY, WI
☐	THE BANDO	ATLANTA, GA
☐	DUFF'S FAMOUS WINGS	NEW YORK, NY
☐	DIRTY BIRDS	SAN DIEGO, CA
☐	NINE-ELEVEN TAVERN	BUFFALO, NY
☐	GRITTY'S	PORTLAND, ME
☐	DELANEY'S HOLE IN THE WALL	NORTH CONWAY, NH

WRITE-IN CANDIDATES

LIQUID ASSETS

AKA: BARS & SPEAKEASIES

NAME OF THE BAR

NUMBER

195

PSST: ADD THIS TO THE INDEX(ES) IN THE BACK SO YOU CAN FIND IT QUICKLY LATER

WHERE WAS IT LOCATED?

CITY: STATE/COUNTRY:

WHY DID YOU COME HERE?

☐ HEARD GREAT THINGS   FORCED AGAINST WILL ☐

☐ IT LOOKED GOOD   KINDA DESPERATE ☐

☐ ONLY THING OPEN   WAS (ALREADY) DRUNK ☐

OTHER:

THE BEST THING(S) YOU HAD:

. . . .

AMBIANCE

① ② ③ ④ ⑤

DRINKS

① ② ③ ④ ⑤

THE WORST THING(S) YOU HAD:

. . . .

SERVICE

① ② ③ ④ ⑤

THE ONE THING YOU'LL NEVER FORGET:

COME HERE AGAIN?   YES ☐   NO ☐   IF DESPERATE ☐

LIQUID ASSETS

NUMBER

196

NAME OF THE BAR

PSST: ADD THIS TO THE INDEX(ES) IN THE BACK SO YOU CAN FIND IT QUICKLY LATER

WHERE WAS IT LOCATED?

CITY: STATE/COUNTRY:

WHY DID YOU COME HERE?

- [ ] HEARD GREAT THINGS
- [ ] IT LOOKED GOOD
- [ ] ONLY THING OPEN

- FORCED AGAINST WILL [ ]
- KINDA DESPERATE [ ]
- WAS (ALREADY) DRUNK [ ]

OTHER:

AMBIANCE
① ② ③ ④ ⑤

DRINKS
① ② ③ ④ ⑤

SERVICE
① ② ③ ④ ⑤

THE BEST THING(S) YOU HAD:

. . . .

THE WORST THING(S) YOU HAD:

. . . .

THE ONE THING YOU'LL NEVER FORGET:

COME HERE AGAIN?   YES [ ]   NO [ ]   IF DESPERATE [ ]

LIQUID ASSETS
AKA: BARS & SPEAKEASIES

NAME OF THE BAR

NUMBER
197

PSST: ADD THIS TO THE INDEX(ES) IN THE BACK SO YOU CAN FIND IT QUICKLY LATER

WHERE WAS IT LOCATED?

CITY: STATE/COUNTRY:

WHY DID YOU COME HERE?

- [ ] HEARD GREAT THINGS
- [ ] IT LOOKED GOOD
- [ ] ONLY THING OPEN
- [ ] FORCED AGAINST WILL
- [ ] KINDA DESPERATE
- [ ] WAS (ALREADY) DRUNK

OTHER:

THE BEST THING(S) YOU HAD:
. . . .

THE WORST THING(S) YOU HAD:
. . . .

AMBIANCE
(1) (2) (3) (4) (5)

DRINKS
(1) (2) (3) (4) (5)

SERVICE
(1) (2) (3) (4) (5)

THE ONE THING YOU'LL NEVER FORGET:

COME HERE AGAIN?   YES [ ]   NO [ ]   IF DESPERATE [ ]

NUMBER

198

NAME OF THE BAR

PSST: ADD THIS TO THE INDEX(ES) IN THE BACK SO YOU CAN FIND IT QUICKLY LATER

WHERE WAS IT LOCATED?

CITY: STATE/COUNTRY:

WHY DID YOU COME HERE?

- [ ] HEARD GREAT THINGS
- [ ] IT LOOKED GOOD
- [ ] ONLY THING OPEN
- [ ] FORCED AGAINST WILL
- [ ] KINDA DESPERATE
- [ ] WAS (ALREADY) DRUNK

OTHER:

AMBIANCE
① ② ③ ④ ⑤

DRINKS
① ② ③ ④ ⑤

SERVICE
① ② ③ ④ ⑤

THE BEST THING(S) YOU HAD:

. . . .

THE WORST THING(S) YOU HAD:

. . . .

THE ONE THING YOU'LL NEVER FORGET:

COME HERE AGAIN?   YES [ ]   NO [ ]   IF DESPERATE [ ]

LIQUID ASSETS

AKA: BARS & SPEAKEASIES

NAME OF THE BAR

NUMBER

199

PSST: ADD THIS TO THE INDEX(ES) IN THE BACK SO YOU CAN FIND IT QUICKLY LATER

WHERE WAS IT LOCATED?

CITY: STATE/COUNTRY:

WHY DID YOU COME HERE?

☐ HEARD GREAT THINGS   FORCED AGAINST WILL ☐
☐ IT LOOKED GOOD   KINDA DESPERATE ☐
☐ ONLY THING OPEN   WAS (ALREADY) DRUNK ☐

OTHER:

THE BEST THING(S) YOU HAD:

AMBIANCE

① ② ③ ④ ⑤

DRINKS

① ② ③ ④ ⑤

THE WORST THING(S) YOU HAD:

SERVICE

① ② ③ ④ ⑤

THE ONE THING YOU'LL NEVER FORGET:

COME HERE AGAIN?   YES ☐   NO ☐   IF DESPERATE ☐

LIQUID ASSETS

NUMBER

200

NAME OF THE BAR

PSST: ADD THIS TO THE INDEX(ES) IN THE BACK SO YOU CAN FIND IT QUICKLY LATER

WHERE WAS IT LOCATED?

CITY: STATE/COUNTRY:

WHY DID YOU COME HERE?

- [ ] HEARD GREAT THINGS
- [ ] IT LOOKED GOOD
- [ ] ONLY THING OPEN
- [ ] FORCED AGAINST WILL
- [ ] KINDA DESPERATE
- [ ] WAS (ALREADY) DRUNK

OTHER:

AMBIANCE
(1) (2) (3) (4) (5)

DRINKS
(1) (2) (3) (4) (5)

SERVICE
(1) (2) (3) (4) (5)

THE BEST THING(S) YOU HAD:

. . . .

THE WORST THING(S) YOU HAD:

. . . .

THE ONE THING YOU'LL NEVER FORGET:

COME HERE AGAIN?   YES [ ]   NO [ ]   IF DESPERATE [ ]

LIQUID ASSETS

AKA: BARS & SPEAKEASIES

NAME OF THE BAR

NUMBER

201

PSST: ADD THIS TO THE INDEX(ES) IN THE BACK SO YOU CAN FIND IT QUICKLY LATER

WHERE WAS IT LOCATED?

CITY: STATE/COUNTRY:

WHY DID YOU COME HERE?

- [ ] HEARD GREAT THINGS
- [ ] IT LOOKED GOOD
- [ ] ONLY THING OPEN
- [ ] FORCED AGAINST WILL
- [ ] KINDA DESPERATE
- [ ] WAS (ALREADY) DRUNK

OTHER:

THE BEST THING(S) YOU HAD:

. . . .

AMBIANCE
① ② ③ ④ ⑤

DRINKS
① ② ③ ④ ⑤

THE WORST THING(S) YOU HAD:

. . . .

SERVICE
① ② ③ ④ ⑤

THE ONE THING YOU'LL NEVER FORGET:

COME HERE AGAIN?   YES [ ]   NO [ ]   IF DESPERATE [ ]

A FEW MUST-TRYS

RESTAURANT	LOCATION
☐ SWORDFISH TOM'S	KANSAS CITY, MO
☐ LUDLOW LIQUORS	CHICAGO, IL
☐ PLEASE DON'T TELL	NEW YORK, NY
☐ BILTONG BAR	ATLANTA, GA
☐ THE GUTTER	NEW YORK, NY
☐ DINO'S	NASHVILLE, TN
☐ HERBS AND RYE	LAS VEGAS, NV
☐ PHOCIFIC STANDARD TIME	SEATTLE, WA
☐ BISOU	PARIS, FRANCE
☐ DOUBLE CHICKEN PLEASE	NEW YORK, NY
☐ PARK BAR	ATLANTA, GA
☐ THUNDERBOLT	LOS ANGELES, CA
☐ CLOVER CLUB	NEW YORK, NY
☐ TELL ME BAR	NEW ORLEANS, LA
☐ THE SHIP*	KANSAS CITY, MO
☐ SISTER LOUISA'S CHURCH.	ATLANTA, MO
☐ PUNCH HOUSE	CHICAGO, IL
☐ OVER UNDER	MIAMI, FL
☐ THE DEAD RABBIT	NEW YORK, NY
☐ MILKY WAY	MONTREAL, CANADA
☐ VINCENT'S	WORCESTER, MA
☐ YACHT CLUB	DENVER, CO
☐ GOODNIGHT SONNY	NEW YORK, NY
☐ EASY TIGER	AUSTIN, TX

WRITE-IN CANDIDATES

*IT'S GREAT–NOT TO MENTION IT'S TWO BLOCKS FROM OUR OFFICE.

LIQUID ASSETS

AKA: BARS & SPEAKEASIES

NAME OF THE BAR

NUMBER

202

PSST: ADD THIS TO THE INDEX(ES) IN THE BACK SO YOU CAN FIND IT QUICKLY LATER

WHERE WAS IT LOCATED?

CITY: STATE/COUNTRY:

WHY DID YOU COME HERE?

- [ ] HEARD GREAT THINGS
- [ ] IT LOOKED GOOD
- [ ] ONLY THING OPEN
- [ ] FORCED AGAINST WILL
- [ ] KINDA DESPERATE
- [ ] WAS (ALREADY) DRUNK

OTHER:

THE BEST THING(S) YOU HAD:

. . . .

THE WORST THING(S) YOU HAD:

. . . .

AMBIANCE
(1) (2) (3) (4) (5)

DRINKS
(1) (2) (3) (4) (5)

SERVICE
(1) (2) (3) (4) (5)

THE ONE THING YOU'LL NEVER FORGET:

COME HERE AGAIN?   YES [ ]   NO [ ]   IF DESPERATE [ ]

LIQUID ASSETS

NUMBER

203

NAME OF THE BAR

PSST: ADD THIS TO THE INDEX(ES) IN THE BACK SO YOU CAN FIND IT QUICKLY LATER

WHERE WAS IT LOCATED?

CITY: STATE/COUNTRY:

WHY DID YOU COME HERE?

- [ ] HEARD GREAT THINGS
- [ ] IT LOOKED GOOD
- [ ] ONLY THING OPEN

- FORCED AGAINST WILL [ ]
- KINDA DESPERATE [ ]
- WAS (ALREADY) DRUNK [ ]

OTHER:

AMBIANCE
① ② ③ ④ ⑤

DRINKS
① ② ③ ④ ⑤

SERVICE
① ② ③ ④ ⑤

THE BEST THING(S) YOU HAD:
. . . .

THE WORST THING(S) YOU HAD:
. . . .

THE ONE THING YOU'LL NEVER FORGET:

COME HERE AGAIN?   YES [ ]   NO [ ]   IF DESPERATE [ ]

LIQUID ASSETS

AKA: BARS & SPEAKEASIES

NAME OF THE BAR

NUMBER

204

PSST: ADD THIS TO THE INDEX(ES) IN THE BACK SO YOU CAN FIND IT QUICKLY LATER

WHERE WAS IT LOCATED?

CITY: STATE/COUNTRY:

WHY DID YOU COME HERE?

- [ ] HEARD GREAT THINGS
- [ ] IT LOOKED GOOD
- [ ] ONLY THING OPEN
- [ ] FORCED AGAINST WILL
- [ ] KINDA DESPERATE
- [ ] WAS (ALREADY) DRUNK

OTHER:

THE BEST THING(S) YOU HAD:

. . . .

THE WORST THING(S) YOU HAD:

. . . .

AMBIANCE
(1) (2) (3) (4) (5)

DRINKS
(1) (2) (3) (4) (5)

SERVICE
(1) (2) (3) (4) (5)

THE ONE THING YOU'LL NEVER FORGET:

COME HERE AGAIN?   YES [ ]   NO [ ]   IF DESPERATE [ ]

LIQUID ASSETS

NUMBER

205

NAME OF THE BAR

PSST: ADD THIS TO THE INDEX(ES) IN THE BACK SO YOU CAN FIND IT QUICKLY LATER

WHERE WAS IT LOCATED?

CITY: STATE/COUNTRY:

WHY DID YOU COME HERE?

- [ ] HEARD GREAT THINGS
- [ ] IT LOOKED GOOD
- [ ] ONLY THING OPEN

- FORCED AGAINST WILL [ ]
- KINDA DESPERATE [ ]
- WAS (ALREADY) DRUNK [ ]

OTHER:

AMBIANCE

① ② ③ ④ ⑤

DRINKS

① ② ③ ④ ⑤

SERVICE

① ② ③ ④ ⑤

THE BEST THING(S) YOU HAD:

. . . .

THE WORST THING(S) YOU HAD:

. . . .

THE ONE THING YOU'LL NEVER FORGET:

COME HERE AGAIN?   YES [ ]   NO [ ]   IF DESPERATE [ ]

LIQUID ASSETS

AKA: BARS & SPEAKEASIES

NAME OF THE BAR

NUMBER

206

PSST: ADD THIS TO THE INDEX(ES) IN THE BACK SO YOU CAN FIND IT QUICKLY LATER

WHERE WAS IT LOCATED?

CITY:

STATE/COUNTRY:

WHY DID YOU COME HERE?

- [ ] HEARD GREAT THINGS
- [ ] IT LOOKED GOOD
- [ ] ONLY THING OPEN
- [ ] FORCED AGAINST WILL
- [ ] KINDA DESPERATE
- [ ] WAS (ALREADY) DRUNK

OTHER:

THE BEST THING(S) YOU HAD:

. . . .

AMBIANCE
① ② ③ ④ ⑤

DRINKS
① ② ③ ④ ⑤

THE WORST THING(S) YOU HAD:

. . . .

SERVICE
① ② ③ ④ ⑤

THE ONE THING YOU'LL NEVER FORGET:

COME HERE AGAIN? YES [ ] NO [ ] IF DESPERATE [ ]

NUMBER

207

NAME OF THE BAR

PSST: ADD THIS TO THE INDEX(ES) IN THE BACK SO YOU CAN FIND IT QUICKLY LATER

WHERE WAS IT LOCATED?

CITY: STATE/COUNTRY:

WHY DID YOU COME HERE?

☐ HEARD GREAT THINGS   FORCED AGAINST WILL ☐

☐ IT LOOKED GOOD   KINDA DESPERATE ☐

☐ ONLY THING OPEN   WAS (ALREADY) DRUNK ☐

OTHER:

AMBIANCE

① ② ③ ④ ⑤

DRINKS

① ② ③ ④ ⑤

SERVICE

① ② ③ ④ ⑤

THE BEST THING(S) YOU HAD:

. . . .

THE WORST THING(S) YOU HAD:

. . . .

THE ONE THING YOU'LL NEVER FORGET:

COME HERE AGAIN?   YES ☐   NO ☐   IF DESPERATE ☐

LIQUID ASSETS

AKA: BARS & SPEAKEASIES

NAME OF THE BAR

NUMBER

208

PSST: ADD THIS TO THE INDEX(ES) IN THE BACK SO YOU CAN FIND IT QUICKLY LATER

WHERE WAS IT LOCATED?

CITY: STATE/COUNTRY:

WHY DID YOU COME HERE?

- [ ] HEARD GREAT THINGS
- [ ] IT LOOKED GOOD
- [ ] ONLY THING OPEN
- [ ] FORCED AGAINST WILL
- [ ] KINDA DESPERATE
- [ ] WAS (ALREADY) DRUNK

OTHER:

THE BEST THING(S) YOU HAD:

. . . .

THE WORST THING(S) YOU HAD:

. . . .

AMBIANCE
(1)(2)(3)(4)(5)

DRINKS
(1)(2)(3)(4)(5)

SERVICE
(1)(2)(3)(4)(5)

THE ONE THING YOU'LL NEVER FORGET:

COME HERE AGAIN?   YES [ ]   NO [ ]   IF DESPERATE [ ]

TAKE A COCKTAIL TOUR

AUSTIN, TX

A COLLECTION OF OUR FAVORITE SPEAKEASIES

AUSTIN-BORN ALCOHOL BRANDS

- ☐ TITO'S VODKA
- ☐ TEXAGAVE BLUE AGAVE
- ☐ PAULA'S TEXAS ORANGE
- ☐ DEEP EDDY VODKA

PSST: HERE'S A BONUS ONE THAT'S THE OPPOSITE OF HIDDEN—THE SIGN BAR. THIS MOSTLY-OUTDOOR BAR IS FILLED WITH HUGE VINTAGE NEON SIGNS FROM THE STORES, BARS, AND RESTAURANTS OF AUSTIN'S PAST.

SPEAKEASY	HIDDEN
☐ MIDNIGHT COWBOY	IN A FORMER BROTHEL
☐ FIREHOUSE LOUNGE	IN A HOSTEL
☐ HERE NOR THERE	DOWN AN ALLEYWAY
☐ SMALL VICTORY	IN A PARKING GARAGE
☐ MEZCALERÍA TOBALÁ	UP A STAIRCASE
☐ RED HEADED STEPCHILD	UNDER AN OLD SIGN
☐ EDEN COCKTAIL ROOM	ACROSS FROM DUMPSTERS
☐ THE TREASURY	DOWN A STAIRCASE
☐ GARAGE	IN A PARKING GARAGE
☐ MILONGA ROOM	IN A BASEMENT
☐ DUMONT'S DOWN LOW	IN A FORMER BROTHEL
☐ EGO'S	IN A PARKING GARAGE
☐ KINFOLK LOUNGE	DOWN A STAIRCASE

WRITE-IN CANDIDATES

LIQUID ASSETS

NAME OF THE BAR

NUMBER

209

PSST: ADD THIS TO THE INDEX(ES) IN THE BACK SO YOU CAN FIND IT QUICKLY LATER

WHERE WAS IT LOCATED?

CITY: STATE/COUNTRY:

WHY DID YOU COME HERE?

- [ ] HEARD GREAT THINGS
- [ ] IT LOOKED GOOD
- [ ] ONLY THING OPEN
- [ ] FORCED AGAINST WILL
- [ ] KINDA DESPERATE
- [ ] WAS (ALREADY) DRUNK

OTHER:

THE BEST THING(S) YOU HAD:

. . . .

THE WORST THING(S) YOU HAD:

. . . .

AMBIANCE
(1) (2) (3) (4) (5)

DRINKS
(1) (2) (3) (4) (5)

SERVICE
(1) (2) (3) (4) (5)

THE ONE THING YOU'LL NEVER FORGET:

COME HERE AGAIN? YES [ ] NO [ ] IF DESPERATE [ ]

NUMBER

210

NAME OF THE BAR

PSST: ADD THIS TO THE INDEX(ES) IN THE BACK SO YOU CAN FIND IT QUICKLY LATER

WHERE WAS IT LOCATED?

CITY: STATE/COUNTRY:

WHY DID YOU COME HERE?

- [ ] HEARD GREAT THINGS
- [ ] IT LOOKED GOOD
- [ ] ONLY THING OPEN

FORCED AGAINST WILL [ ]
KINDA DESPERATE [ ]
WAS (ALREADY) DRUNK [ ]

OTHER:

AMBIANCE
① ② ③ ④ ⑤

THE BEST THING(S) YOU HAD:
. . . .

DRINKS
① ② ③ ④ ⑤

THE WORST THING(S) YOU HAD:
. . . .

SERVICE
① ② ③ ④ ⑤

THE ONE THING YOU'LL NEVER FORGET:

COME HERE AGAIN?   YES [ ]   NO [ ]   IF DESPERATE [ ]

SWEET RELIEF

SWEET RELIEF

AKA: ICE CREAM & DESSERTS

NAME OF THE RESTAURANT

NUMBER

211

PSST: ADD THIS TO THE INDEX(ES) IN THE BACK SO YOU CAN FIND IT QUICKLY LATER

WHERE WAS IT LOCATED?

CITY: STATE/COUNTRY:

WHY DID YOU EAT HERE?

☐ HEARD GREAT THINGS   FORCED AGAINST WILL ☐

☐ IT LOOKED GOOD   HUNGRY & DESPERATE ☐

☐ ONLY THING OPEN   WAS DRUNK ☐

OTHER:

THE BEST THING(S) YOU ATE:

. . . .

AMBIANCE
① ② ③ ④ ⑤

FOOD
① ② ③ ④ ⑤

THE WORST THING(S) YOU ATE:

. . . .

SERVICE
① ② ③ ④ ⑤

THE ONE THING YOU'LL NEVER FORGET:

EAT HERE AGAIN?   YES ☐   NO ☐   IF DESPERATE ☐

SWEET RELIEF

NUMBER
212

NAME OF THE RESTAURANT

PSST: ADD THIS TO THE INDEX(ES) IN THE BACK SO YOU CAN FIND IT QUICKLY LATER

WHERE WAS IT LOCATED?

CITY: STATE/COUNTRY:

WHY DID YOU EAT HERE?

- [ ] HEARD GREAT THINGS
- [ ] IT LOOKED GOOD
- [ ] ONLY THING OPEN
- [ ] FORCED AGAINST WILL
- [ ] HUNGRY & DESPERATE
- [ ] WAS DRUNK

OTHER:

AMBIANCE
① ② ③ ④ ⑤

FOOD
① ② ③ ④ ⑤

SERVICE
① ② ③ ④ ⑤

THE BEST THING(S) YOU ATE:
. . . .

THE WORST THING(S) YOU ATE:
. . . .

THE ONE THING YOU'LL NEVER FORGET:

EAT HERE AGAIN?   YES [ ]   NO [ ]   IF DESPERATE [ ]

SWEET RELIEF

NAME OF THE RESTAURANT

NUMBER

213

PSST: ADD THIS TO THE INDEX(ES) IN THE BACK SO YOU CAN FIND IT QUICKLY LATER

WHERE WAS IT LOCATED?

CITY: STATE/COUNTRY:

WHY DID YOU EAT HERE?

- [ ] HEARD GREAT THINGS
- [ ] IT LOOKED GOOD
- [ ] ONLY THING OPEN

- [ ] FORCED AGAINST WILL
- [ ] HUNGRY & DESPERATE
- [ ] WAS DRUNK

OTHER:

THE BEST THING(S) YOU ATE:

. . . .

THE WORST THING(S) YOU ATE:

. . . .

AMBIANCE
① ② ③ ④ ⑤

FOOD
① ② ③ ④ ⑤

SERVICE
① ② ③ ④ ⑤

THE ONE THING YOU'LL NEVER FORGET:

EAT HERE AGAIN?   YES [ ]   NO [ ]   IF DESPERATE [ ]

SWEET RELIEF

NUMBER

214

NAME OF THE RESTAURANT

PSST: ADD THIS TO THE INDEX(ES) IN THE BACK SO YOU CAN FIND IT QUICKLY LATER

WHERE WAS IT LOCATED?

CITY:

STATE/COUNTRY:

WHY DID YOU EAT HERE?

- [ ] HEARD GREAT THINGS
- [ ] IT LOOKED GOOD
- [ ] ONLY THING OPEN
- [ ] FORCED AGAINST WILL
- [ ] HUNGRY & DESPERATE
- [ ] WAS DRUNK

OTHER:

AMBIANCE
① ② ③ ④ ⑤

FOOD
① ② ③ ④ ⑤

SERVICE
① ② ③ ④ ⑤

THE BEST THING(S) YOU ATE:

. . . .

THE WORST THING(S) YOU ATE:

. . . .

THE ONE THING YOU'LL NEVER FORGET:

EAT HERE AGAIN?   YES [ ]   NO [ ]   IF DESPERATE [ ]

SWEET RELIEF

AKA: ICE CREAM & DESSERTS

NAME OF THE RESTAURANT

NUMBER

215

PSST: ADD THIS TO THE INDEX(ES) IN THE BACK SO YOU CAN FIND IT QUICKLY LATER

WHERE WAS IT LOCATED?

CITY: STATE/COUNTRY:

WHY DID YOU EAT HERE?

- [ ] HEARD GREAT THINGS
- [ ] IT LOOKED GOOD
- [ ] ONLY THING OPEN
- [ ] FORCED AGAINST WILL
- [ ] HUNGRY & DESPERATE
- [ ] WAS DRUNK

OTHER:

THE BEST THING(S) YOU ATE:

. . . .

AMBIANCE
① ② ③ ④ ⑤

FOOD
① ② ③ ④ ⑤

THE WORST THING(S) YOU ATE:

. . . .

SERVICE
① ② ③ ④ ⑤

THE ONE THING YOU'LL NEVER FORGET:

EAT HERE AGAIN?   YES [ ]   NO [ ]   IF DESPERATE [ ]

SWEET RELIEF

NUMBER
216

NAME OF THE RESTAURANT

PSST: ADD THIS TO THE INDEX(ES) IN THE BACK SO YOU CAN FIND IT QUICKLY LATER

WHERE WAS IT LOCATED?

CITY: STATE/COUNTRY:

WHY DID YOU EAT HERE?

- [ ] HEARD GREAT THINGS
- [ ] IT LOOKED GOOD
- [ ] ONLY THING OPEN
- [ ] FORCED AGAINST WILL
- [ ] HUNGRY & DESPERATE
- [ ] WAS DRUNK

OTHER:

AMBIANCE
① ② ③ ④ ⑤

FOOD
① ② ③ ④ ⑤

SERVICE
① ② ③ ④ ⑤

THE BEST THING(S) YOU ATE:
. . . .

THE WORST THING(S) YOU ATE:
. . . .

THE ONE THING YOU'LL NEVER FORGET:

EAT HERE AGAIN?   YES [ ]   NO [ ]   IF DESPERATE [ ]

SWEET RELIEF

AKA: ICE CREAM & DESSERTS

NAME OF THE RESTAURANT

NUMBER

217

PSST: ADD THIS TO THE INDEX(ES) IN THE BACK SO YOU CAN FIND IT QUICKLY LATER

WHERE WAS IT LOCATED?

CITY: STATE/COUNTRY:

WHY DID YOU EAT HERE?

- [ ] HEARD GREAT THINGS
- [ ] IT LOOKED GOOD
- [ ] ONLY THING OPEN
- [ ] FORCED AGAINST WILL
- [ ] HUNGRY & DESPERATE
- [ ] WAS DRUNK

OTHER:

THE BEST THING(S) YOU ATE:

. . . .

THE WORST THING(S) YOU ATE:

. . . .

AMBIANCE
(1) (2) (3) (4) (5)

FOOD
(1) (2) (3) (4) (5)

SERVICE
(1) (2) (3) (4) (5)

THE ONE THING YOU'LL NEVER FORGET:

EAT HERE AGAIN?   YES [ ]   NO [ ]   IF DESPERATE [ ]

☐ BEEN THERE # BLACKHOLE BAKERY

5531 TROOST AVE, KANSAS CITY, MO 64110

A FEW FAVORITES

☐ MOCHI DONUTS

☐ BRIOCHE CINNAMON ROLL

☐ BLUEBERRY CROISSANT

WAKING UP EARLY
① ② ③ ④ ⑤

BEING WORTH IT
① ② ③ ④ ⑤ (5 circled)

WHILE THIS PLACE IS KNOWN (RIGHTFULLY SO) FOR THEIR INCREDIBLE MOCHI DONUTS—EVERY PASTRY THAT THEY MAKE IS TOP-NOTCH. THE ONLY THING IS, YOU HAVE TO BE THERE WHEN THEY OPEN (IF NOT EARLIER) TO EVEN STAND A CHANCE OF GETTING ANY OF THEM. THEY SELL OUT IMMEDIATELY. ANYWAY, BACK TO THOSE MOCHI DONUTS. EACH ONE IS A BALL, A BIT SMALLER THAN A BASEBALL—PERFECT FOR EATING LIKE A SUGARY APPLE. PSST: THE FLAVORS CHANGE ALMOST DAILY.

☐ BEEN THERE # BIG GAY ICE CREAM

516 COLUMBUS AVE, NEW YORK, NY 10024

A FEW FAVORITES

☐ THE SALTY PIMP CONE

☐ THE BEA ARTHER CONE

☐ THE MONDAY SUNDAE

BIGNESS
① ② ③ ④ ⑤

GAYNESS
① ② ③ ④ ⑤ (5 circled)

WHILE THE ORIGINAL LOCATION IN THE WEST VILLAGE CLOSED DURING THE PANDEMIC—YOU CAN THANKFULLY STILL ENJOY THIS TINY ICE CREAM SPOT ON THE UPPER WEST SIDE. USING SOFT-SERVE AS THE BASE FOR THEIR DIPPED CONES, THEY SMOTHER THEM IN INVENTIVE (AND DELICIOUS) TOPPINGS—AND GIVE THEM NAMES LIKE 'THE SALTY PIMP.' PLUS, A PORTION OF THEIR PROFITS GOES TOWARDS LOCAL LGBTQ+ CAUSES—WHICH MAKES THE ICE CREAM TASTE EVEN BETTER.

SWEET RELIEF

AKA: ICE CREAM & DESSERTS

NAME OF THE RESTAURANT

NUMBER

218

PSST: ADD THIS TO THE INDEX(ES) IN THE BACK SO YOU CAN FIND IT QUICKLY LATER

WHERE WAS IT LOCATED?

CITY: STATE/COUNTRY:

WHY DID YOU EAT HERE?

- [ ] HEARD GREAT THINGS
- [ ] IT LOOKED GOOD
- [ ] ONLY THING OPEN
- [ ] FORCED AGAINST WILL
- [ ] HUNGRY & DESPERATE
- [ ] WAS DRUNK

OTHER:

THE BEST THING(S) YOU ATE:

. . . .

THE WORST THING(S) YOU ATE:

. . . .

AMBIANCE
① ② ③ ④ ⑤

FOOD
① ② ③ ④ ⑤

SERVICE
① ② ③ ④ ⑤

THE ONE THING YOU'LL NEVER FORGET:

EAT HERE AGAIN?   YES [ ]   NO [ ]   IF DESPERATE [ ]

SWEET RELIEF

NUMBER

219

NAME OF THE RESTAURANT

PSST: ADD THIS TO THE INDEX(ES) IN THE BACK SO YOU CAN FIND IT QUICKLY LATER

WHERE WAS IT LOCATED?

CITY: STATE/COUNTRY:

WHY DID YOU EAT HERE?

- [ ] HEARD GREAT THINGS
- [ ] IT LOOKED GOOD
- [ ] ONLY THING OPEN

- FORCED AGAINST WILL [ ]
- HUNGRY & DESPERATE [ ]
- WAS DRUNK [ ]

OTHER:

AMBIANCE
(1) (2) (3) (4) (5)

FOOD
(1) (2) (3) (4) (5)

SERVICE
(1) (2) (3) (4) (5)

THE BEST THING(S) YOU ATE:
. . . .

THE WORST THING(S) YOU ATE:
. . . .

THE ONE THING YOU'LL NEVER FORGET:

EAT HERE AGAIN?   YES [ ]   NO [ ]   IF DESPERATE [ ]

SWEET RELIEF

AKA: ICE CREAM & DESSERTS

NAME OF THE RESTAURANT

NUMBER

220

PSST: ADD THIS TO THE INDEX(ES) IN THE BACK SO YOU CAN FIND IT QUICKLY LATER

WHERE WAS IT LOCATED?

CITY: STATE/COUNTRY:

WHY DID YOU EAT HERE?

- [ ] HEARD GREAT THINGS
- [ ] IT LOOKED GOOD
- [ ] ONLY THING OPEN
- [ ] FORCED AGAINST WILL
- [ ] HUNGRY & DESPERATE
- [ ] WAS DRUNK

OTHER:

THE BEST THING(S) YOU ATE:

. . . .

THE WORST THING(S) YOU ATE:

. . . .

AMBIANCE
① ② ③ ④ ⑤

FOOD
① ② ③ ④ ⑤

SERVICE
① ② ③ ④ ⑤

THE ONE THING YOU'LL NEVER FORGET:

EAT HERE AGAIN?   YES [ ]   NO [ ]   IF DESPERATE [ ]

NUMBER

221

NAME OF THE RESTAURANT

PSST: ADD THIS TO THE INDEX(ES) IN THE BACK SO YOU CAN FIND IT QUICKLY LATER

WHERE WAS IT LOCATED?

CITY: STATE/COUNTRY:

WHY DID YOU EAT HERE?

- [ ] HEARD GREAT THINGS
- [ ] IT LOOKED GOOD
- [ ] ONLY THING OPEN

FORCED AGAINST WILL [ ]
HUNGRY & DESPERATE [ ]
WAS DRUNK [ ]

OTHER:

AMBIANCE
(1) (2) (3) (4) (5)

FOOD
(1) (2) (3) (4) (5)

SERVICE
(1) (2) (3) (4) (5)

THE BEST THING(S) YOU ATE:

. . . .

THE WORST THING(S) YOU ATE:

. . . .

THE ONE THING YOU'LL NEVER FORGET:

EAT HERE AGAIN?   YES [ ]   NO [ ]   IF DESPERATE [ ]

SWEET RELIEF

NAME OF THE RESTAURANT

NUMBER

222

PSST: ADD THIS TO THE INDEX(ES) IN THE BACK SO YOU CAN FIND IT QUICKLY LATER

WHERE WAS IT LOCATED?

CITY: STATE/COUNTRY:

WHY DID YOU EAT HERE?

☐ HEARD GREAT THINGS   FORCED AGAINST WILL ☐

☐ IT LOOKED GOOD   HUNGRY & DESPERATE ☐

☐ ONLY THING OPEN   WAS DRUNK ☐

OTHER:

THE BEST THING(S) YOU ATE:

. . . .

THE WORST THING(S) YOU ATE:

. . . .

AMBIANCE
① ② ③ ④ ⑤

FOOD
① ② ③ ④ ⑤

SERVICE
① ② ③ ④ ⑤

THE ONE THING YOU'LL NEVER FORGET:

EAT HERE AGAIN?   YES ☐   NO ☐   IF DESPERATE ☐

SWEET RELIEF

NUMBER

223

NAME OF THE RESTAURANT

PSST: ADD THIS TO THE INDEX(ES) IN THE BACK SO YOU CAN FIND IT QUICKLY LATER

WHERE WAS IT LOCATED?

CITY: STATE/COUNTRY:

WHY DID YOU EAT HERE?

- [ ] HEARD GREAT THINGS
- [ ] IT LOOKED GOOD
- [ ] ONLY THING OPEN
- [ ] FORCED AGAINST WILL
- [ ] HUNGRY & DESPERATE
- [ ] WAS DRUNK

OTHER:

AMBIANCE
① ② ③ ④ ⑤

FOOD
① ② ③ ④ ⑤

SERVICE
① ② ③ ④ ⑤

THE BEST THING(S) YOU ATE:

. . . .

THE WORST THING(S) YOU ATE:

. . . .

THE ONE THING YOU'LL NEVER FORGET:

EAT HERE AGAIN? YES [ ] NO [ ] IF DESPERATE [ ]

SWEET RELIEF

AKA: ICE CREAM & DESSERTS

NAME OF THE RESTAURANT

NUMBER

224

PSST: ADD THIS TO THE INDEX(ES) IN THE BACK SO YOU CAN FIND IT QUICKLY LATER

WHERE WAS IT LOCATED?

CITY:

STATE/COUNTRY:

WHY DID YOU EAT HERE?

- [ ] HEARD GREAT THINGS
- [ ] IT LOOKED GOOD
- [ ] ONLY THING OPEN
- [ ] FORCED AGAINST WILL
- [ ] HUNGRY & DESPERATE
- [ ] WAS DRUNK

OTHER:

THE BEST THING(S) YOU ATE:

. . . .

THE WORST THING(S) YOU ATE:

. . . .

AMBIANCE
(1) (2) (3) (4) (5)

FOOD
(1) (2) (3) (4) (5)

SERVICE
(1) (2) (3) (4) (5)

THE ONE THING YOU'LL NEVER FORGET:

EAT HERE AGAIN?   YES [ ]   NO [ ]   IF DESPERATE [ ]

ICE CREAM

NATIONAL ICE CREAM DAY IS THE THIRD SUNDAY IN JULY

PERFECT FOR	TERRIBLE FOR
☐ EATING WHEN HAPPY	AVOIDING CALORIES ☐
☐ EATING WHEN SAD	AVOIDING CHILDREN ☐

'ICE CREAM HEADACHES' ARE CAUSED WHEN THE BODY SENSES A SUDDEN, EXTREMELY COLD TEMPERATURE IN THE THROAT OR MOUTH. IN ORDER TO 'SOLVE' THIS, BLOOD VESSELS IN THE HEAD QUICKLY EXPAND TO LET EXTRA BLOOD IN FOR WARMTH. IT'S THE CHANGE IN BLOOD VESSEL SIZE THAT CAUSES UNEXPECTED PAIN.

FIND NOTABLES AT: LOCATION

☐ FRYCE CREAM	NASHVILLE, TN
☐ HUMPHRY SLOCOMBE	SAN FRANCISCO, CA
☐ CONEFLOWER CREAMERY	OMAHA, NE
☐ CHINATOWN ICE CREAM FACTORY	NEW YORK, NY
☐ TRICYCLE ICE CREAM	PROVIDENCE, RI
☐ FIFTY LICKS ICE CREAM	PORTLAND, OR
☐ BI-RITE CREAMERY	SAN FRANCISCO, CA
☐ AN'S DRY CLEANING	SAN DIEGO, CA
☐ SUNDAES AND CONES	NEW YORK, NY
☐ THE BENT SPOON	PRINCETON, NJ
☐ MOLLY MOON'S	SEATTLE, WA
☐ CRANK & BOOM	LEXINGTON, KY

WRITE-IN CANDIDATES

SWEET RELIEF
AKA: ICE CREAM & DESSERTS

NAME OF THE RESTAURANT

NUMBER

225

PSST: ADD THIS TO THE INDEX(ES) IN THE BACK SO YOU CAN FIND IT QUICKLY LATER

WHERE WAS IT LOCATED?

CITY:

STATE/COUNTRY:

WHY DID YOU EAT HERE?

- [ ] HEARD GREAT THINGS
- [ ] IT LOOKED GOOD
- [ ] ONLY THING OPEN
- [ ] FORCED AGAINST WILL
- [ ] HUNGRY & DESPERATE
- [ ] WAS DRUNK

OTHER:

THE BEST THING(S) YOU ATE:

. . . .

THE WORST THING(S) YOU ATE:

. . . .

AMBIANCE
(1) (2) (3) (4) (5)

FOOD
(1) (2) (3) (4) (5)

SERVICE
(1) (2) (3) (4) (5)

THE ONE THING YOU'LL NEVER FORGET:

EAT HERE AGAIN?   YES [ ]   NO [ ]   IF DESPERATE [ ]

SWEET RELIEF

NUMBER

226

NAME OF THE RESTAURANT

PSST: ADD THIS TO THE INDEX(ES) IN THE BACK SO YOU CAN FIND IT QUICKLY LATER

WHERE WAS IT LOCATED?

CITY: STATE/COUNTRY:

WHY DID YOU EAT HERE?

- [ ] HEARD GREAT THINGS
- [ ] IT LOOKED GOOD
- [ ] ONLY THING OPEN
- [ ] FORCED AGAINST WILL
- [ ] HUNGRY & DESPERATE
- [ ] WAS DRUNK

OTHER:

AMBIANCE
(1) (2) (3) (4) (5)

FOOD
(1) (2) (3) (4) (5)

SERVICE
(1) (2) (3) (4) (5)

THE BEST THING(S) YOU ATE:

. . . .

THE WORST THING(S) YOU ATE:

. . . .

THE ONE THING YOU'LL NEVER FORGET:

EAT HERE AGAIN?   YES [ ]   NO [ ]   IF DESPERATE [ ]

SWEET RELIEF

AKA: ICE CREAM & DESSERTS

NAME OF THE RESTAURANT

NUMBER

227

PSST: ADD THIS TO THE INDEX(ES) IN THE BACK SO YOU CAN FIND IT QUICKLY LATER

WHERE WAS IT LOCATED?

CITY: STATE/COUNTRY:

WHY DID YOU EAT HERE?

- [ ] HEARD GREAT THINGS
- [ ] IT LOOKED GOOD
- [ ] ONLY THING OPEN
- [ ] FORCED AGAINST WILL
- [ ] HUNGRY & DESPERATE
- [ ] WAS DRUNK

OTHER:

THE BEST THING(S) YOU ATE:

. . . .

AMBIANCE
(1) (2) (3) (4) (5)

FOOD
(1) (2) (3) (4) (5)

THE WORST THING(S) YOU ATE:

. . . .

SERVICE
(1) (2) (3) (4) (5)

THE ONE THING YOU'LL NEVER FORGET:

EAT HERE AGAIN?   YES [ ]   NO [ ]   IF DESPERATE [ ]

SWEET RELIEF

NUMBER

228

NAME OF THE RESTAURANT

PSST: ADD THIS TO THE INDEX(ES) IN THE BACK SO YOU CAN FIND IT QUICKLY LATER

WHERE WAS IT LOCATED?

CITY: STATE/COUNTRY:

WHY DID YOU EAT HERE?

- [ ] HEARD GREAT THINGS
- [ ] IT LOOKED GOOD
- [ ] ONLY THING OPEN
- [ ] FORCED AGAINST WILL
- [ ] HUNGRY & DESPERATE
- [ ] WAS DRUNK

OTHER:

AMBIANCE
① ② ③ ④ ⑤

FOOD
① ② ③ ④ ⑤

SERVICE
① ② ③ ④ ⑤

THE BEST THING(S) YOU ATE:
. . . .

THE WORST THING(S) YOU ATE:
. . . .

THE ONE THING YOU'LL NEVER FORGET:

EAT HERE AGAIN?   YES [ ] NO [ ] IF DESPERATE [ ]

SWEET RELIEF

AKA: ICE CREAM & DESSERTS

NAME OF THE RESTAURANT

NUMBER

229

PSST: ADD THIS TO THE INDEX(ES) IN THE BACK SO YOU CAN FIND IT QUICKLY LATER

WHERE WAS IT LOCATED?

CITY: STATE/COUNTRY:

WHY DID YOU EAT HERE?

- [ ] HEARD GREAT THINGS
- [ ] IT LOOKED GOOD
- [ ] ONLY THING OPEN
- [ ] FORCED AGAINST WILL
- [ ] HUNGRY & DESPERATE
- [ ] WAS DRUNK

OTHER:

THE BEST THING(S) YOU ATE:

. . . .

THE WORST THING(S) YOU ATE:

. . . .

AMBIANCE
(1) (2) (3) (4) (5)

FOOD
(1) (2) (3) (4) (5)

SERVICE
(1) (2) (3) (4) (5)

THE ONE THING YOU'LL NEVER FORGET:

EAT HERE AGAIN?   YES [ ]   NO [ ]   IF DESPERATE [ ]

SWEET RELIEF

NUMBER

230

NAME OF THE RESTAURANT

PSST: ADD THIS TO THE INDEX(ES) IN THE BACK SO YOU CAN FIND IT QUICKLY LATER

WHERE WAS IT LOCATED?

CITY: STATE/COUNTRY:

WHY DID YOU EAT HERE?

- [ ] HEARD GREAT THINGS
- [ ] IT LOOKED GOOD
- [ ] ONLY THING OPEN
- [ ] FORCED AGAINST WILL
- [ ] HUNGRY & DESPERATE
- [ ] WAS DRUNK

OTHER:

AMBIANCE
(1)(2)(3)(4)(5)

FOOD
(1)(2)(3)(4)(5)

SERVICE
(1)(2)(3)(4)(5)

THE BEST THING(S) YOU ATE:
. . . .

THE WORST THING(S) YOU ATE:
. . . .

THE ONE THING YOU'LL NEVER FORGET:

EAT HERE AGAIN?   YES [ ]   NO [ ]   IF DESPERATE [ ]

SWEET RELIEF

AKA: ICE CREAM & DESSERTS

NAME OF THE RESTAURANT

NUMBER

231

PSST: ADD THIS TO THE INDEX(ES) IN THE BACK SO YOU CAN FIND IT QUICKLY LATER

WHERE WAS IT LOCATED?

CITY: STATE/COUNTRY:

WHY DID YOU EAT HERE?

- [ ] HEARD GREAT THINGS
- [ ] IT LOOKED GOOD
- [ ] ONLY THING OPEN
- [ ] FORCED AGAINST WILL
- [ ] HUNGRY & DESPERATE
- [ ] WAS DRUNK

OTHER:

THE BEST THING(S) YOU ATE:

. . . .

AMBIANCE
① ② ③ ④ ⑤

FOOD
① ② ③ ④ ⑤

THE WORST THING(S) YOU ATE:

. . . .

SERVICE
① ② ③ ④ ⑤

THE ONE THING YOU'LL NEVER FORGET:

EAT HERE AGAIN? YES [ ] NO [ ] IF DESPERATE [ ]

A FEW MUST-TRYS

RESTAURANT	LOCATION
☐ BAILEY'S CHOCOLATE BAR	ST. LOUIS, MO
☐ JOJO'S SHAVE ICE	KAUAI, HI
☐ PASTICHE FINE DESSERTS	PROVIDENCE, RI
☐ HOT LICKS HOMEMADE ICE CREAM	FAIRBANKS, AK
☐ EDWARD'S DESSERT KITCHEN	MINNEAPOLIS, MN
☐ LABADIE'S BAKERY	LEWISTON, ME
☐ ST. FRANCIS FOUNTAIN	SAN FRANCISCO, CA
☐ KAKAWA CHOCOLATE HOUSE	SANTA FE, NM
☐ KERMIT'S KEY LIME SHOPPE	KEY WEST, FL
☐ CROWN CANDY KITCHEN	ST. LOUIS, MO
☐ VACCARO'S ITALIAN PASTRY SHOP	BALTIMORE, MD
☐ MINDY'S BAKERY	CHICAGO, IL
☐ NORA CUPCAKE COMPANY	MIDDLETOWN, CT
☐ BEILER'S BAKERY	PHILADELPHIA, PA
☐ D BAR	DENVER, CO
☐ FLOUR BAKERY + CAFÉ	BOSTON, MA
☐ B SWEET DESSERT BAR	LOS ANGELES, CA
☐ POPOVERS ON THE SQUARE	PORTSMOUTH, NH
☐ CAFÉ DU MONDE	NEW ORLEANS, LA
☐ LEVAIN BAKERY	NEW YORK, NY
☐ MIKE'S PASTRY	BOSTON, MA
☐ MARKHAM & FITZ CHOCOLATE	BENTONVILLE, AR
☐ DOMINIQUE ANSEL BAKERY	NEW YORK, NY
☐ OLLIE'S FINE ICE CREAM*	DELAWARE, OH

WRITE-IN CANDIDATES

*IT'S NO LONGER THERE—BUT IT WAS MY DAD'S AND IT WAS GREAT.

SWEET RELIEF
AKA: ICE CREAM & DESSERTS

NAME OF THE RESTAURANT

NUMBER

232

PSST: ADD THIS TO THE INDEX(ES) IN THE BACK SO YOU CAN FIND IT QUICKLY LATER

WHERE WAS IT LOCATED?

CITY: STATE/COUNTRY:

WHY DID YOU EAT HERE?

- [ ] HEARD GREAT THINGS
- [ ] IT LOOKED GOOD
- [ ] ONLY THING OPEN
- [ ] FORCED AGAINST WILL
- [ ] HUNGRY & DESPERATE
- [ ] WAS DRUNK

OTHER:

THE BEST THING(S) YOU ATE:

....

AMBIANCE
(1) (2) (3) (4) (5)

FOOD
(1) (2) (3) (4) (5)

THE WORST THING(S) YOU ATE:

....

SERVICE
(1) (2) (3) (4) (5)

THE ONE THING YOU'LL NEVER FORGET:

EAT HERE AGAIN?   YES [ ]   NO [ ]   IF DESPERATE [ ]

NUMBER

233

NAME OF THE RESTAURANT

PSST: ADD THIS TO THE INDEX(ES) IN THE BACK SO YOU CAN FIND IT QUICKLY LATER

WHERE WAS IT LOCATED?

CITY: STATE/COUNTRY:

WHY DID YOU EAT HERE?

- [ ] HEARD GREAT THINGS
- [ ] IT LOOKED GOOD
- [ ] ONLY THING OPEN

FORCED AGAINST WILL [ ]
HUNGRY & DESPERATE [ ]
WAS DRUNK [ ]

OTHER:

AMBIANCE
① ② ③ ④ ⑤

FOOD
① ② ③ ④ ⑤

SERVICE
① ② ③ ④ ⑤

THE BEST THING(S) YOU ATE:
. . . .

THE WORST THING(S) YOU ATE:
. . . .

THE ONE THING YOU'LL NEVER FORGET:

EAT HERE AGAIN?   YES [ ]   NO [ ]   IF DESPERATE [ ]

SWEET RELIEF

AKA: ICE CREAM & DESSERTS

NAME OF THE RESTAURANT

NUMBER

234

PSST: ADD THIS TO THE INDEX(ES) IN THE BACK SO YOU CAN FIND IT QUICKLY LATER

WHERE WAS IT LOCATED?

CITY: STATE/COUNTRY:

WHY DID YOU EAT HERE?

- [ ] HEARD GREAT THINGS
- [ ] IT LOOKED GOOD
- [ ] ONLY THING OPEN
- [ ] FORCED AGAINST WILL
- [ ] HUNGRY & DESPERATE
- [ ] WAS DRUNK

OTHER:

THE BEST THING(S) YOU ATE:

. . . .

THE WORST THING(S) YOU ATE:

. . . .

AMBIANCE
(1)(2)(3)(4)(5)

FOOD
(1)(2)(3)(4)(5)

SERVICE
(1)(2)(3)(4)(5)

THE ONE THING YOU'LL NEVER FORGET:

EAT HERE AGAIN?   YES [ ]   NO [ ]   IF DESPERATE [ ]

SWEET RELIEF

NUMBER

235

NAME OF THE RESTAURANT

PSST: ADD THIS TO THE INDEX(ES) IN THE BACK SO YOU CAN FIND IT QUICKLY LATER

WHERE WAS IT LOCATED?

CITY: STATE/COUNTRY:

WHY DID YOU EAT HERE?

- [ ] HEARD GREAT THINGS
- [ ] IT LOOKED GOOD
- [ ] ONLY THING OPEN

- FORCED AGAINST WILL [ ]
- HUNGRY & DESPERATE [ ]
- WAS DRUNK [ ]

OTHER:

AMBIANCE
(1) (2) (3) (4) (5)

FOOD
(1) (2) (3) (4) (5)

SERVICE
(1) (2) (3) (4) (5)

THE BEST THING(S) YOU ATE:

. . . .

THE WORST THING(S) YOU ATE:

. . . .

THE ONE THING YOU'LL NEVER FORGET:

EAT HERE AGAIN?   YES [ ]   NO [ ]   IF DESPERATE [ ]

SWEET RELIEF

AKA: ICE CREAM & DESSERTS

NAME OF THE RESTAURANT

NUMBER

236

PSST: ADD THIS TO THE INDEX(ES) IN THE BACK SO YOU CAN FIND IT QUICKLY LATER

WHERE WAS IT LOCATED?

CITY: STATE/COUNTRY:

WHY DID YOU EAT HERE?

- [ ] HEARD GREAT THINGS
- [ ] IT LOOKED GOOD
- [ ] ONLY THING OPEN
- [ ] FORCED AGAINST WILL
- [ ] HUNGRY & DESPERATE
- [ ] WAS DRUNK

OTHER:

THE BEST THING(S) YOU ATE:

. . . .

THE WORST THING(S) YOU ATE:

. . . .

AMBIANCE
(1) (2) (3) (4) (5)

FOOD
(1) (2) (3) (4) (5)

SERVICE
(1) (2) (3) (4) (5)

THE ONE THING YOU'LL NEVER FORGET:

EAT HERE AGAIN?   YES [ ]   NO [ ]   IF DESPERATE [ ]

NUMBER

237

NAME OF THE RESTAURANT

PSST: ADD THIS TO THE INDEX(ES) IN THE BACK SO YOU CAN FIND IT QUICKLY LATER

WHERE WAS IT LOCATED?

CITY: STATE/COUNTRY:

WHY DID YOU EAT HERE?

☐ HEARD GREAT THINGS   FORCED AGAINST WILL ☐
☐ IT LOOKED GOOD   HUNGRY & DESPERATE ☐
☐ ONLY THING OPEN   WAS DRUNK ☐

OTHER:

AMBIANCE
① ② ③ ④ ⑤

FOOD
① ② ③ ④ ⑤

SERVICE
① ② ③ ④ ⑤

THE BEST THING(S) YOU ATE:

. . . .

THE WORST THING(S) YOU ATE:

. . . .

THE ONE THING YOU'LL NEVER FORGET:

EAT HERE AGAIN?   YES ☐   NO ☐   IF DESPERATE ☐

SWEET RELIEF

AKA: ICE CREAM & DESSERTS

NAME OF THE RESTAURANT

NUMBER

238

PSST: ADD THIS TO THE INDEX(ES) IN THE BACK SO YOU CAN FIND IT QUICKLY LATER

WHERE WAS IT LOCATED?

CITY: STATE/COUNTRY:

WHY DID YOU EAT HERE?

- [ ] HEARD GREAT THINGS
- [ ] IT LOOKED GOOD
- [ ] ONLY THING OPEN
- [ ] FORCED AGAINST WILL
- [ ] HUNGRY & DESPERATE
- [ ] WAS DRUNK

OTHER:

THE BEST THING(S) YOU ATE:

. . . .

THE WORST THING(S) YOU ATE:

. . . .

AMBIANCE
(1) (2) (3) (4) (5)

FOOD
(1) (2) (3) (4) (5)

SERVICE
(1) (2) (3) (4) (5)

THE ONE THING YOU'LL NEVER FORGET:

EAT HERE AGAIN?   YES [ ]   NO [ ]   IF DESPERATE [ ]

MIAMI, FL

HAS THE MOST DESSERT SHOPS PER SQUARE MILE (USA)

LOCAL DESSERT SPECIALTIES

- [ ] KEY LIME PIE
- [ ] PASTELITOS DE GUAYABA
- [ ] SWEET POTATO PUDDING
- [ ] PIÑA ASADA

IN 1965, THE STATE OF FLORIDA INTRODUCED A BILL THAT WOULD HAVE CALLED FOR A $100 FINE AGAINST ANYONE ADVERTISING KEY LIME PIES NOT MADE WITH ACTUAL KEY LIMES. IT DIDN'T PASS.

RESTAURANT	KNOWN FOR
[ ] DBAKERS SWEET STUDIO	MACARON SANDWICHES
[ ] TAIYAKI	MATCHA SOFT SERVE
[ ] CINDY LOU'S COOKIES	SPECIALTY COOKIES
[ ] PIONONOS	PAVLOVA CAKE
[ ] AZUCAR	CUBAN ICE CREAM
[ ] CRY BABY CREAMERY	ICE CREAM SANDWICHES
[ ] BOCAS HOUSE	SPECIALTY MILKSHAKES
[ ] BACHOUR	BEAUTIFUL PASTRIES
[ ] NIGHT OWL COOKIES	SPECIALTY COOKIES
[ ] FIREMAN DEREK'S BAKE SHOP	KEY LIME PIE
[ ] BIANCO GELATO	NATURAL GELATO
[ ] THE SALTY DONUT	SPECIALTY DONUTS
[ ] MADRUGA BAKERY	LEMON POLENTA CAKE

WRITE-IN CANDIDATES

SWEET RELIEF

NAME OF THE RESTAURANT

NUMBER

239

PSST: ADD THIS TO THE INDEX(ES) IN THE BACK SO YOU CAN FIND IT QUICKLY LATER

WHERE WAS IT LOCATED?

CITY: STATE/COUNTRY:

WHY DID YOU EAT HERE?

☐ HEARD GREAT THINGS   FORCED AGAINST WILL ☐

☐ IT LOOKED GOOD   HUNGRY & DESPERATE ☐

☐ ONLY THING OPEN   WAS DRUNK ☐

OTHER:

THE BEST THING(S) YOU ATE:

. . . .

THE WORST THING(S) YOU ATE:

. . . .

AMBIANCE
① ② ③ ④ ⑤

FOOD
① ② ③ ④ ⑤

SERVICE
① ② ③ ④ ⑤

THE ONE THING YOU'LL NEVER FORGET:

EAT HERE AGAIN?   YES ☐   NO ☐   IF DESPERATE ☐

SWEET RELIEF

NUMBER

240

NAME OF THE RESTAURANT

PSST: ADD THIS TO THE INDEX(ES) IN THE BACK SO YOU CAN FIND IT QUICKLY LATER

WHERE WAS IT LOCATED?

CITY: STATE/COUNTRY:

WHY DID YOU EAT HERE?

- [ ] HEARD GREAT THINGS
- [ ] IT LOOKED GOOD
- [ ] ONLY THING OPEN

- FORCED AGAINST WILL [ ]
- HUNGRY & DESPERATE [ ]
- WAS DRUNK [ ]

OTHER:

AMBIANCE
(1) (2) (3) (4) (5)

FOOD
(1) (2) (3) (4) (5)

SERVICE
(1) (2) (3) (4) (5)

THE BEST THING(S) YOU ATE:

. . . .

THE WORST THING(S) YOU ATE:

. . . .

THE ONE THING YOU'LL NEVER FORGET:

EAT HERE AGAIN?   YES [ ]   NO [ ]   IF DESPERATE [ ]

FOOD FOR THOUGHT

THE BEST OF ALABAMA

NUMBER   RESTAURANT

① ② ③ ④ ⑤ RATING   CITY

① ② ③ ④ ⑤ RATING   CITY

① ② ③ ④ ⑤ RATING   CITY

① ② ③ ④ ⑤ RATING   CITY

① ② ③ ④ ⑤ RATING   CITY

① ② ③ ④ ⑤ RATING   CITY

① ② ③ ④ ⑤ RATING   CITY

RESTAURANT **NUMBER**

CITY RATING ① ② ③ ④ ⑤

CITY RATING ① ② ③ ④ ⑤

CITY RATING ① ② ③ ④ ⑤

CITY RATING ① ② ③ ④ ⑤

CITY RATING ① ② ③ ④ ⑤

CITY RATING ① ② ③ ④ ⑤

CITY RATING ① ② ③ ④ ⑤

THE BEST OF ARIZONA

NUMBER　　　　　　　　　　　　　　**RESTAURANT**

① ② ③ ④ ⑤　RATING　　　　　　　　　CITY

① ② ③ ④ ⑤　RATING　　　　　　　　　CITY

① ② ③ ④ ⑤　RATING　　　　　　　　　CITY

① ② ③ ④ ⑤　RATING　　　　　　　　　CITY

① ② ③ ④ ⑤　RATING　　　　　　　　　CITY

① ② ③ ④ ⑤　RATING　　　　　　　　　CITY

① ② ③ ④ ⑤　RATING　　　　　　　　　CITY

THE BEST OF ARKANSAS

RESTAURANT

NUMBER

CITY

RATING (1) (2) (3) (4) (5)

CITY

RATING (1) (2) (3) (4) (5)

CITY

RATING (1) (2) (3) (4) (5)

CITY

RATING (1) (2) (3) (4) (5)

CITY

RATING (1) (2) (3) (4) (5)

CITY

RATING (1) (2) (3) (4) (5)

CITY

RATING (1) (2) (3) (4) (5)

THE BEST OF CALIFORNIA

NUMBER   **RESTAURANT**

① ② ③ ④ ⑤ RATING   CITY

① ② ③ ④ ⑤ RATING   CITY

① ② ③ ④ ⑤ RATING   CITY

① ② ③ ④ ⑤ RATING   CITY

① ② ③ ④ ⑤ RATING   CITY

① ② ③ ④ ⑤ RATING   CITY

① ② ③ ④ ⑤ RATING   CITY

THE BEST OF COLORADO

RESTAURANT **NUMBER**

CITY RATING (1)(2)(3)(4)(5)

CITY RATING (1)(2)(3)(4)(5)

CITY RATING (1)(2)(3)(4)(5)

CITY RATING (1)(2)(3)(4)(5)

CITY RATING (1)(2)(3)(4)(5)

CITY RATING (1)(2)(3)(4)(5)

CITY RATING (1)(2)(3)(4)(5)

THE BEST OF CONNECTICUT

NUMBER   **RESTAURANT**

(1) (2) (3) (4) (5) RATING   CITY

(1) (2) (3) (4) (5) RATING   CITY

(1) (2) (3) (4) (5) RATING   CITY

(1) (2) (3) (4) (5) RATING   CITY

(1) (2) (3) (4) (5) RATING   CITY

(1) (2) (3) (4) (5) RATING   CITY

(1) (2) (3) (4) (5) RATING   CITY

RESTAURANT

NUMBER

CITY RATING ① ② ③ ④ ⑤

CITY RATING ① ② ③ ④ ⑤

CITY RATING ① ② ③ ④ ⑤

CITY RATING ① ② ③ ④ ⑤

CITY RATING ① ② ③ ④ ⑤

CITY RATING ① ② ③ ④ ⑤

CITY RATING ① ② ③ ④ ⑤

THE BEST OF FLORIDA

NUMBER

RESTAURANT

① ② ③ ④ ⑤ RATING

CITY

NUMBER

RESTAURANT

① ② ③ ④ ⑤ RATING

CITY

① ② ③ ④ ⑤ RATING

CITY

① ② ③ ④ ⑤ RATING

CITY

① ② ③ ④ ⑤ RATING

CITY

① ② ③ ④ ⑤ RATING

CITY

① ② ③ ④ ⑤ RATING

CITY

RESTAURANT

NUMBER

CITY RATING ① ② ③ ④ ⑤

RESTAURANT

NUMBER

CITY RATING ① ② ③ ④ ⑤

CITY RATING ① ② ③ ④ ⑤

CITY RATING ① ② ③ ④ ⑤

CITY RATING ① ② ③ ④ ⑤

CITY RATING ① ② ③ ④ ⑤

CITY RATING ① ② ③ ④ ⑤

THE BEST OF HAWAII

NUMBER

RESTAURANT

① ② ③ ④ ⑤ RATING

CITY

① ② ③ ④ ⑤ RATING

CITY

① ② ③ ④ ⑤ RATING

CITY

① ② ③ ④ ⑤ RATING

CITY

① ② ③ ④ ⑤ RATING

CITY

① ② ③ ④ ⑤ RATING

CITY

① ② ③ ④ ⑤ RATING

CITY

RESTAURANT

NUMBER

CITY

RATING ① ② ③ ④ ⑤

RESTAURANT

NUMBER

CITY

RATING ① ② ③ ④ ⑤

RESTAURANT

NUMBER

CITY

RATING ① ② ③ ④ ⑤

RESTAURANT

NUMBER

CITY

RATING ① ② ③ ④ ⑤

RESTAURANT

NUMBER

CITY

RATING ① ② ③ ④ ⑤

RESTAURANT

NUMBER

CITY

RATING ① ② ③ ④ ⑤

RESTAURANT

NUMBER

CITY

RATING ① ② ③ ④ ⑤

THE BEST OF ILLINOIS

NUMBER

RESTAURANT

(1) (2) (3) (4) (5) RATING

CITY

(1) (2) (3) (4) (5) RATING

CITY

(1) (2) (3) (4) (5) RATING

CITY

(1) (2) (3) (4) (5) RATING

CITY

(1) (2) (3) (4) (5) RATING

CITY

(1) (2) (3) (4) (5) RATING

CITY

(1) (2) (3) (4) (5) RATING

CITY

RESTAURANT

NUMBER

....

CITY   RATING ① ② ③ ④ ⑤

....

CITY   RATING ① ② ③ ④ ⑤

....

CITY   RATING ① ② ③ ④ ⑤

....

CITY   RATING ① ② ③ ④ ⑤

....

CITY   RATING ① ② ③ ④ ⑤

....

CITY   RATING ① ② ③ ④ ⑤

....

CITY   RATING ① ② ③ ④ ⑤

THE BEST OF IOWA

NUMBER

RESTAURANT

① ② ③ ④ ⑤ RATING

CITY

① ② ③ ④ ⑤ RATING

CITY

① ② ③ ④ ⑤ RATING

CITY

① ② ③ ④ ⑤ RATING

CITY

① ② ③ ④ ⑤ RATING

CITY

① ② ③ ④ ⑤ RATING

CITY

① ② ③ ④ ⑤ RATING

CITY

THE BEST OF KANSAS

RESTAURANT   **NUMBER**

CITY   RATING ① ② ③ ④ ⑤

CITY   RATING ① ② ③ ④ ⑤

CITY   RATING ① ② ③ ④ ⑤

CITY   RATING ① ② ③ ④ ⑤

CITY   RATING ① ② ③ ④ ⑤

CITY   RATING ① ② ③ ④ ⑤

CITY   RATING ① ② ③ ④ ⑤

THE BEST OF KENTUCKY

NUMBER   RESTAURANT

①②③④⑤ RATING   CITY

NUMBER   RESTAURANT

①②③④⑤ RATING   CITY

NUMBER   RESTAURANT

①②③④⑤ RATING   CITY

NUMBER   RESTAURANT

①②③④⑤ RATING   CITY

NUMBER   RESTAURANT

①②③④⑤ RATING   CITY

NUMBER   RESTAURANT

①②③④⑤ RATING   CITY

NUMBER   RESTAURANT

①②③④⑤ RATING   CITY

RESTAURANT

NUMBER

CITY

RATING ① ② ③ ④ ⑤

CITY

RATING ① ② ③ ④ ⑤

CITY

RATING ① ② ③ ④ ⑤

CITY

RATING ① ② ③ ④ ⑤

CITY

RATING ① ② ③ ④ ⑤

CITY

RATING ① ② ③ ④ ⑤

CITY

RATING ① ② ③ ④ ⑤

THE BEST OF MAINE

NUMBER

RESTAURANT

① ② ③ ④ ⑤ RATING   CITY

NUMBER

① ② ③ ④ ⑤ RATING   CITY

① ② ③ ④ ⑤ RATING   CITY

① ② ③ ④ ⑤ RATING   CITY

① ② ③ ④ ⑤ RATING   CITY

① ② ③ ④ ⑤ RATING   CITY

① ② ③ ④ ⑤ RATING   CITY

RESTAURANT

NUMBER

CITY

RATING (1) (2) (3) (4) (5)

CITY

RATING (1) (2) (3) (4) (5)

CITY

RATING (1) (2) (3) (4) (5)

CITY

RATING (1) (2) (3) (4) (5)

CITY

RATING (1) (2) (3) (4) (5)

CITY

RATING (1) (2) (3) (4) (5)

CITY

RATING (1) (2) (3) (4) (5)

THE BEST OF MASSACHUSETTS

NUMBER   **RESTAURANT**

① ② ③ ④ ⑤ RATING   CITY

① ② ③ ④ ⑤ RATING   CITY

① ② ③ ④ ⑤ RATING   CITY

① ② ③ ④ ⑤ RATING   CITY

① ② ③ ④ ⑤ RATING   CITY

① ② ③ ④ ⑤ RATING   CITY

① ② ③ ④ ⑤ RATING   CITY

THE BEST OF MICHIGAN

RESTAURANT

NUMBER

CITY

RATING ① ② ③ ④ ⑤

CITY

RATING ① ② ③ ④ ⑤

CITY

RATING ① ② ③ ④ ⑤

CITY

RATING ① ② ③ ④ ⑤

CITY

RATING ① ② ③ ④ ⑤

CITY

RATING ① ② ③ ④ ⑤

CITY

RATING ① ② ③ ④ ⑤

THE BEST OF MINNESOTA

NUMBER   RESTAURANT

① ② ③ ④ ⑤ RATING   CITY

① ② ③ ④ ⑤ RATING   CITY

① ② ③ ④ ⑤ RATING   CITY

① ② ③ ④ ⑤ RATING   CITY

① ② ③ ④ ⑤ RATING   CITY

① ② ③ ④ ⑤ RATING   CITY

① ② ③ ④ ⑤ RATING   CITY

THE BEST OF MISSISSIPPI

RESTAURANT | NUMBER

CITY | RATING (1)(2)(3)(4)(5)

CITY | RATING (1)(2)(3)(4)(5)

CITY | RATING (1)(2)(3)(4)(5)

CITY | RATING (1)(2)(3)(4)(5)

CITY | RATING (1)(2)(3)(4)(5)

CITY | RATING (1)(2)(3)(4)(5)

CITY | RATING (1)(2)(3)(4)(5)

THE BEST OF MISSOURI

NUMBER   RESTAURANT

① ② ③ ④ ⑤ RATING   CITY

① ② ③ ④ ⑤ RATING   CITY

① ② ③ ④ ⑤ RATING   CITY

① ② ③ ④ ⑤ RATING   CITY

① ② ③ ④ ⑤ RATING   CITY

① ② ③ ④ ⑤ RATING   CITY

① ② ③ ④ ⑤ RATING   CITY

RESTAURANT   **NUMBER**

CITY   RATING ① ② ③ ④ ⑤

CITY   RATING ① ② ③ ④ ⑤

CITY   RATING ① ② ③ ④ ⑤

CITY   RATING ① ② ③ ④ ⑤

CITY   RATING ① ② ③ ④ ⑤

CITY   RATING ① ② ③ ④ ⑤

CITY   RATING ① ② ③ ④ ⑤

THE BEST OF NEBRASKA

NUMBER   **RESTAURANT**

① ② ③ ④ ⑤ RATING   CITY

① ② ③ ④ ⑤ RATING   CITY

① ② ③ ④ ⑤ RATING   CITY

① ② ③ ④ ⑤ RATING   CITY

① ② ③ ④ ⑤ RATING   CITY

① ② ③ ④ ⑤ RATING   CITY

① ② ③ ④ ⑤ RATING   CITY

RESTAURANT **NUMBER**

. . . .

CITY RATING ① ② ③ ④ ⑤

. . . .

CITY RATING ① ② ③ ④ ⑤

. . . .

CITY RATING ① ② ③ ④ ⑤

. . . .

CITY RATING ① ② ③ ④ ⑤

. . . .

CITY RATING ① ② ③ ④ ⑤

. . . .

CITY RATING ① ② ③ ④ ⑤

. . . .

CITY RATING ① ② ③ ④ ⑤

THE BEST OF NEW HAMPSHIRE

NUMBER   **RESTAURANT**

① ② ③ ④ ⑤ RATING   CITY

① ② ③ ④ ⑤ RATING   CITY

① ② ③ ④ ⑤ RATING   CITY

① ② ③ ④ ⑤ RATING   CITY

① ② ③ ④ ⑤ RATING   CITY

① ② ③ ④ ⑤ RATING   CITY

① ② ③ ④ ⑤ RATING   CITY

THE BEST OF NEW JERSEY

RESTAURANT   **NUMBER**

CITY   RATING ① ② ③ ④ ⑤

CITY   RATING ① ② ③ ④ ⑤

CITY   RATING ① ② ③ ④ ⑤

CITY   RATING ① ② ③ ④ ⑤

CITY   RATING ① ② ③ ④ ⑤

CITY   RATING ① ② ③ ④ ⑤

CITY   RATING ① ② ③ ④ ⑤

THE BEST OF NEW MEXICO

NUMBER | RESTAURANT

① ② ③ ④ ⑤ RATING | CITY

① ② ③ ④ ⑤ RATING | CITY

① ② ③ ④ ⑤ RATING | CITY

① ② ③ ④ ⑤ RATING | CITY

① ② ③ ④ ⑤ RATING | CITY

① ② ③ ④ ⑤ RATING | CITY

① ② ③ ④ ⑤ RATING | CITY

THE BEST OF NEW YORK

RESTAURANT   NUMBER

CITY   RATING ① ② ③ ④ ⑤

CITY   RATING ① ② ③ ④ ⑤

CITY   RATING ① ② ③ ④ ⑤

CITY   RATING ① ② ③ ④ ⑤

CITY   RATING ① ② ③ ④ ⑤

CITY   RATING ① ② ③ ④ ⑤

CITY   RATING ① ② ③ ④ ⑤

THE BEST OF NORTH CAROLINA

NUMBER   **RESTAURANT**

① ② ③ ④ ⑤ RATING   CITY

① ② ③ ④ ⑤ RATING   CITY

① ② ③ ④ ⑤ RATING   CITY

① ② ③ ④ ⑤ RATING   CITY

① ② ③ ④ ⑤ RATING   CITY

① ② ③ ④ ⑤ RATING   CITY

① ② ③ ④ ⑤ RATING   CITY

THE BEST OF NORTH DAKOTA

RESTAURANT　　　　　　　　　　　　　　**NUMBER**

CITY　　　　　　　　　　RATING ① ② ③ ④ ⑤

CITY　　　　　　　　　　RATING ① ② ③ ④ ⑤

CITY　　　　　　　　　　RATING ① ② ③ ④ ⑤

CITY　　　　　　　　　　RATING ① ② ③ ④ ⑤

CITY　　　　　　　　　　RATING ① ② ③ ④ ⑤

CITY　　　　　　　　　　RATING ① ② ③ ④ ⑤

CITY　　　　　　　　　　RATING ① ② ③ ④ ⑤

THE BEST OF OHIO

NUMBER   **RESTAURANT**

(1) (2) (3) (4) (5) RATING   CITY

(1) (2) (3) (4) (5) RATING   CITY

(1) (2) (3) (4) (5) RATING   CITY

(1) (2) (3) (4) (5) RATING   CITY

(1) (2) (3) (4) (5) RATING   CITY

(1) (2) (3) (4) (5) RATING   CITY

(1) (2) (3) (4) (5) RATING   CITY

THE BEST OF OKLAHOMA

RESTAURANT

NUMBER

CITY

RATING (1)(2)(3)(4)(5)

NUMBER

CITY

RATING (1)(2)(3)(4)(5)

CITY

RATING (1)(2)(3)(4)(5)

CITY

RATING (1)(2)(3)(4)(5)

CITY

RATING (1)(2)(3)(4)(5)

CITY

RATING (1)(2)(3)(4)(5)

CITY

RATING (1)(2)(3)(4)(5)

THE BEST OF OREGON

NUMBER   **RESTAURANT**

(1) (2) (3) (4) (5)   RATING   CITY

(1) (2) (3) (4) (5)   RATING   CITY

(1) (2) (3) (4) (5)   RATING   CITY

(1) (2) (3) (4) (5)   RATING   CITY

(1) (2) (3) (4) (5)   RATING   CITY

(1) (2) (3) (4) (5)   RATING   CITY

(1) (2) (3) (4) (5)   RATING   CITY

THE BEST OF PENNSYLVANIA

RESTAURANT	NUMBER
CITY	RATING ① ② ③ ④ ⑤

RESTAURANT	NUMBER
CITY	RATING ① ② ③ ④ ⑤

RESTAURANT	NUMBER
CITY	RATING ① ② ③ ④ ⑤

RESTAURANT	NUMBER
CITY	RATING ① ② ③ ④ ⑤

RESTAURANT	NUMBER
CITY	RATING ① ② ③ ④ ⑤

	NUMBER
CITY	RATING ① ② ③ ④ ⑤

	NUMBER
CITY	RATING ① ② ③ ④ ⑤

THE BEST OF RHODE ISLAND

NUMBER | RESTAURANT

(1) (2) (3) (4) (5) RATING | CITY

(1) (2) (3) (4) (5) RATING | CITY

(1) (2) (3) (4) (5) RATING | CITY

(1) (2) (3) (4) (5) RATING | CITY

(1) (2) (3) (4) (5) RATING | CITY

(1) (2) (3) (4) (5) RATING | CITY

(1) (2) (3) (4) (5) RATING | CITY

THE BEST OF SOUTH CAROLINA

RESTAURANT

NUMBER

CITY

RATING ① ② ③ ④ ⑤

NUMBER

CITY

RATING ① ② ③ ④ ⑤

NUMBER

CITY

RATING ① ② ③ ④ ⑤

NUMBER

CITY

RATING ① ② ③ ④ ⑤

NUMBER

CITY

RATING ① ② ③ ④ ⑤

NUMBER

CITY

RATING ① ② ③ ④ ⑤

NUMBER

CITY

RATING ① ② ③ ④ ⑤

THE BEST OF SOUTH DAKOTA

NUMBER   RESTAURANT

① ② ③ ④ ⑤ RATING   CITY

① ② ③ ④ ⑤ RATING   CITY

① ② ③ ④ ⑤ RATING   CITY

① ② ③ ④ ⑤ RATING   CITY

① ② ③ ④ ⑤ RATING   CITY

① ② ③ ④ ⑤ RATING   CITY

① ② ③ ④ ⑤ RATING   CITY

THE BEST OF TENNESSEE

RESTAURANT   **NUMBER**

CITY   RATING ① ② ③ ④ ⑤

CITY   RATING ① ② ③ ④ ⑤

CITY   RATING ① ② ③ ④ ⑤

CITY   RATING ① ② ③ ④ ⑤

CITY   RATING ① ② ③ ④ ⑤

CITY   RATING ① ② ③ ④ ⑤

CITY   RATING ① ② ③ ④ ⑤

THE BEST OF TEXAS

NUMBER

RESTAURANT

① ② ③ ④ ⑤ RATING

CITY

① ② ③ ④ ⑤ RATING

CITY

① ② ③ ④ ⑤ RATING

CITY

① ② ③ ④ ⑤ RATING

CITY

① ② ③ ④ ⑤ RATING

CITY

① ② ③ ④ ⑤ RATING

CITY

① ② ③ ④ ⑤ RATING

CITY

RESTAURANT NUMBER

CITY RATING ① ② ③ ④ ⑤

CITY RATING ① ② ③ ④ ⑤

CITY RATING ① ② ③ ④ ⑤

CITY RATING ① ② ③ ④ ⑤

CITY RATING ① ② ③ ④ ⑤

CITY RATING ① ② ③ ④ ⑤

CITY RATING ① ② ③ ④ ⑤

THE BEST OF VERMONT

NUMBER   **RESTAURANT**

① ② ③ ④ ⑤ RATING   CITY

① ② ③ ④ ⑤ RATING   CITY

① ② ③ ④ ⑤ RATING   CITY

① ② ③ ④ ⑤ RATING   CITY

① ② ③ ④ ⑤ RATING   CITY

① ② ③ ④ ⑤ RATING   CITY

① ② ③ ④ ⑤ RATING   CITY

RESTAURANT   **NUMBER**

CITY   RATING ① ② ③ ④ ⑤

CITY   RATING ① ② ③ ④ ⑤

CITY   RATING ① ② ③ ④ ⑤

CITY   RATING ① ② ③ ④ ⑤

CITY   RATING ① ② ③ ④ ⑤

CITY   RATING ① ② ③ ④ ⑤

CITY   RATING ① ② ③ ④ ⑤

THE BEST OF WASHINGTON

NUMBER   **RESTAURANT**

① ② ③ ④ ⑤ RATING   CITY

① ② ③ ④ ⑤ RATING   CITY

① ② ③ ④ ⑤ RATING   CITY

① ② ③ ④ ⑤ RATING   CITY

① ② ③ ④ ⑤ RATING   CITY

① ② ③ ④ ⑤ RATING   CITY

① ② ③ ④ ⑤ RATING   CITY

THE BEST OF WASHINGTON D.C.

RESTAURANT

NUMBER

....

ADDRESS

RATING (1)(2)(3)(4)(5)

....

ADDRESS

RATING (1)(2)(3)(4)(5)

....

ADDRESS

RATING (1)(2)(3)(4)(5)

....

ADDRESS

RATING (1)(2)(3)(4)(5)

....

ADDRESS

RATING (1)(2)(3)(4)(5)

....

ADDRESS

RATING (1)(2)(3)(4)(5)

....

ADDRESS

RATING (1)(2)(3)(4)(5)

THE BEST OF WEST VIRGINIA

NUMBER   **RESTAURANT**

① ② ③ ④ ⑤ RATING   CITY

① ② ③ ④ ⑤ RATING   CITY

① ② ③ ④ ⑤ RATING   CITY

① ② ③ ④ ⑤ RATING   CITY

① ② ③ ④ ⑤ RATING   CITY

① ② ③ ④ ⑤ RATING   CITY

① ② ③ ④ ⑤ RATING   CITY

RESTAURANT NUMBER

. . . .
CITY RATING ① ② ③ ④ ⑤

. . . .
CITY RATING ① ② ③ ④ ⑤

. . . .
CITY RATING ① ② ③ ④ ⑤

. . . .
CITY RATING ① ② ③ ④ ⑤

. . . .
CITY RATING ① ② ③ ④ ⑤

. . . .
CITY RATING ① ② ③ ④ ⑤

. . . .
CITY RATING ① ② ③ ④ ⑤

THE BEST OF WYOMING

NUMBER   **RESTAURANT**

① ② ③ ④ ⑤ RATING   CITY

① ② ③ ④ ⑤ RATING   CITY

① ② ③ ④ ⑤ RATING   CITY

① ② ③ ④ ⑤ RATING   CITY

① ② ③ ④ ⑤ RATING   CITY

① ② ③ ④ ⑤ RATING   CITY

① ② ③ ④ ⑤ RATING   CITY

THE BEST OF THE WORLD

RESTAURANT

NUMBER

LOCATION   RATING ① ② ③ ④ ⑤

LOCATION   RATING ① ② ③ ④ ⑤

LOCATION   RATING ① ② ③ ④ ⑤

LOCATION   RATING ① ② ③ ④ ⑤

LOCATION   RATING ① ② ③ ④ ⑤

LOCATION   RATING ① ② ③ ④ ⑤

LOCATION   RATING ① ② ③ ④ ⑤

FAVORITE BARBECUE PLACES

NUMBER   **RESTAURANT**

(1) (2) (3) (4) (5)   RATING   LOCATION

(1) (2) (3) (4) (5)   RATING   LOCATION

(1) (2) (3) (4) (5)   RATING   LOCATION

(1) (2) (3) (4) (5)   RATING   LOCATION

(1) (2) (3) (4) (5)   RATING   LOCATION

(1) (2) (3) (4) (5)   RATING   LOCATION

(1) (2) (3) (4) (5)   RATING   LOCATION

FAVORITE CHINESE PLACES

RESTAURANT

NUMBER

LOCATION

RATING ① ② ③ ④ ⑤

LOCATION

RATING ① ② ③ ④ ⑤

LOCATION

RATING ① ② ③ ④ ⑤

LOCATION

RATING ① ② ③ ④ ⑤

LOCATION

RATING ① ② ③ ④ ⑤

LOCATION

RATING ① ② ③ ④ ⑤

LOCATION

RATING ① ② ③ ④ ⑤

FAVORITE GREEK PLACES

NUMBER   RESTAURANT

(1) (2) (3) (4) (5) RATING   LOCATION

(1) (2) (3) (4) (5) RATING   LOCATION

(1) (2) (3) (4) (5) RATING   LOCATION

(1) (2) (3) (4) (5) RATING   LOCATION

(1) (2) (3) (4) (5) RATING   LOCATION

(1) (2) (3) (4) (5) RATING   LOCATION

(1) (2) (3) (4) (5) RATING   LOCATION

FAVORITE INDIAN PLACES

RESTAURANT   NUMBER

LOCATION   RATING (1)(2)(3)(4)(5)

LOCATION   RATING (1)(2)(3)(4)(5)

LOCATION   RATING (1)(2)(3)(4)(5)

LOCATION   RATING (1)(2)(3)(4)(5)

LOCATION   RATING (1)(2)(3)(4)(5)

LOCATION   RATING (1)(2)(3)(4)(5)

LOCATION   RATING (1)(2)(3)(4)(5)

FAVORITE ITALIAN PLACES

NUMBER   **RESTAURANT**

① ② ③ ④ ⑤ RATING   LOCATION

① ② ③ ④ ⑤ RATING   LOCATION

① ② ③ ④ ⑤ RATING   LOCATION

① ② ③ ④ ⑤ RATING   LOCATION

① ② ③ ④ ⑤ RATING   LOCATION

① ② ③ ④ ⑤ RATING   LOCATION

① ② ③ ④ ⑤ RATING   LOCATION

FAVORITE JAPANESE PLACES

RESTAURANT　　　　　　　　　　　　　　　**NUMBER**

LOCATION　　　　　　　RATING ① ② ③ ④ ⑤

LOCATION　　　　　　　RATING ① ② ③ ④ ⑤

LOCATION　　　　　　　RATING ① ② ③ ④ ⑤

LOCATION　　　　　　　RATING ① ② ③ ④ ⑤

LOCATION　　　　　　　RATING ① ② ③ ④ ⑤

LOCATION　　　　　　　RATING ① ② ③ ④ ⑤

LOCATION　　　　　　　RATING ① ② ③ ④ ⑤

FAVORITE KOREAN PLACES

NUMBER   RESTAURANT

①②③④⑤ RATING   LOCATION

①②③④⑤ RATING   LOCATION

①②③④⑤ RATING   LOCATION

①②③④⑤ RATING   LOCATION

①②③④⑤ RATING   LOCATION

①②③④⑤ RATING   LOCATION

①②③④⑤ RATING   LOCATION

FAVORITE MEXICAN PLACES

RESTAURANT   NUMBER

LOCATION   RATING ① ② ③ ④ ⑤

LOCATION   RATING ① ② ③ ④ ⑤

LOCATION   RATING ① ② ③ ④ ⑤

LOCATION   RATING ① ② ③ ④ ⑤

LOCATION   RATING ① ② ③ ④ ⑤

LOCATION   RATING ① ② ③ ④ ⑤

LOCATION   RATING ① ② ③ ④ ⑤

FAVORITE SEAFOOD PLACES

NUMBER   **RESTAURANT**

(1) (2) (3) (4) (5) **RATING**   **LOCATION**

(1) (2) (3) (4) (5) **RATING**   **LOCATION**

(1) (2) (3) (4) (5) **RATING**   **LOCATION**

(1) (2) (3) (4) (5) **RATING**   **LOCATION**

(1) (2) (3) (4) (5) **RATING**   **LOCATION**

(1) (2) (3) (4) (5) **RATING**   **LOCATION**

(1) (2) (3) (4) (5) **RATING**   **LOCATION**

FAVORITE THAI PLACES

RESTAURANT　　　　　　　　　　　　　　**NUMBER**

LOCATION　　　　　　　RATING ① ② ③ ④ ⑤

LOCATION　　　　　　　RATING ① ② ③ ④ ⑤

LOCATION　　　　　　　RATING ① ② ③ ④ ⑤

LOCATION　　　　　　　RATING ① ② ③ ④ ⑤

LOCATION　　　　　　　RATING ① ② ③ ④ ⑤

LOCATION　　　　　　　RATING ① ② ③ ④ ⑤

LOCATION　　　　　　　RATING ① ② ③ ④ ⑤

FAVORITE VEGETARIAN PLACES

NUMBER

RESTAURANT

① ② ③ ④ ⑤ RATING

LOCATION

① ② ③ ④ ⑤ RATING

LOCATION

① ② ③ ④ ⑤ RATING

LOCATION

① ② ③ ④ ⑤ RATING

LOCATION

① ② ③ ④ ⑤ RATING

LOCATION

① ② ③ ④ ⑤ RATING

LOCATION

① ② ③ ④ ⑤ RATING

LOCATION

FAVORITE VIETNAMESE PLACES

RESTAURANT

NUMBER

LOCATION RATING ① ② ③ ④ ⑤

LOCATION RATING ① ② ③ ④ ⑤

LOCATION RATING ① ② ③ ④ ⑤

LOCATION RATING ① ② ③ ④ ⑤

LOCATION RATING ① ② ③ ④ ⑤

LOCATION RATING ① ② ③ ④ ⑤

LOCATION RATING ① ② ③ ④ ⑤

BRASSMONKEYGOODS.COM

✖

@BRASSMONKEYGOODS 📷

ISBN: 978-0-7353-8105-6